KU-070-283

INSIGHT POCKET GUIDE

IRELAND

APA PUBLICATIONS

Part of the Langenscheidt Publishing Group

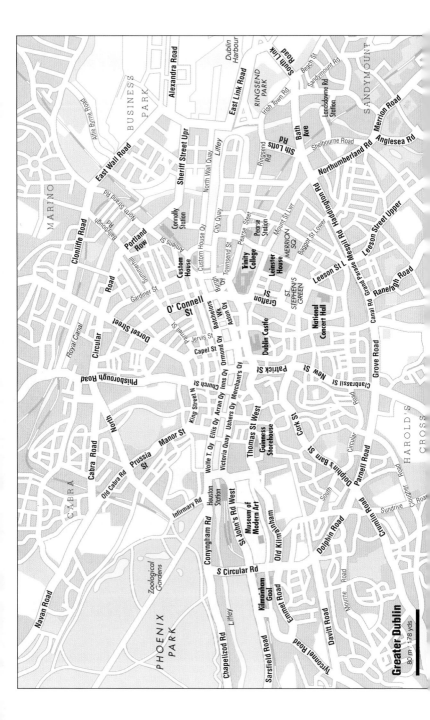

Greater Dublin

80 m / 178 yds

introduction

Welcome

T his guidebook combines the interests and enthusiasms of two of the world's best-known information providers: Insight Guides, who have set the standard for visual travel guides since 1970, and Discovery Channel, the world's premier source of non-fiction television programming. Its aim is to bring you the best of the Emerald Isle in a series of tailor-made itineraries devised by Insight's correspondent in Ireland, Guy Mansell.

The 17 itineraries in this book cater to a variety of time frames and tastes, and are selected to focus on the most fascinating regions and cultural aspects for visitors in the Republic of Ireland. Whether you fancy exploring the Guinness Brewery in Dublin, abbeys and Megalithic sites, or landscapes immortalised by W.B. Yeats, there is a route here to suit you. Supporting the itineraries are sections on history and culture, nightlife, shopping, as well as a calendar of events, and all the practical information you'll need to plan your trip, including recommended hotels, pubs and restaurants.

 Guy Mansell was delighted to write this Pocket Guide. It was, he says, an opportunity to share one of his enduring passions with people who, by the very act of choosing to come here, were likely to love the Irish landscapes and delight in its rich oral, literary and musical traditions. But as one of its best-known native sons, George Bernard Shaw, pointed out, Ireland is not simply a place, but rather a state of mind: it is romantic, passionate, garrulous. Here a stranger fast becomes a friend thanks to one of the chief pleasures of the Irish, conversation. Mansell offers his readers one piece of advice: 'Do not think you have to complete all of these itineraries and thus make a mad dash across the land under the ayatollah of clock time. Relax, reflect and remember that, in the words of the wise old proverb, 'there is as much to see in a blade of grass as in the whole meadow'.

HISTORY AND CULTURE

The arrival of the Celts, the invasion of the Normans, the Battle of the Boyne and the road to independence – a brief account of major events in Ireland's history................**11**

ITINERARIES

These itineraries concentrate on the highlights of the Republic of Ireland. They are divided into five areas: Dublin and surroundings, the northwest, the far west, the southwest and the southeast. For restaurant and accommodation listings, *see pages 73–76 and 86–89.*

DUBLIN

THE NORTHWEST

THE FAR WEST

Preceding pages: west coast vista near Caherdaniel
Following pages: Ireland has a great pub scene

History & Culture

A huge number of antiquities and ancient ruins litter the itineraries in this book. This is hardly surprising, as the history of Ireland has been written on the land for millennia. This small island contains some 130,000 monuments and, with aerial surveying, the count is increasing all the time.

The first signs of man in Ireland date from the Mesolithic era, some 8,000 years ago. Ireland was never under the auspices of the Roman Empire and the remains of her early peoples were left alone. Today this attracts archaeologists from all over the world to visit, dig and study. What little scholars know, they have inferred from the ways in which the dead were buried and the artefacts found in tombs. There is nothing here as grand as the pyramids of the ancient pharaohs, although the huge burial mounds at Newgrange, Knowth and Dowth must have been awesome to behold in 2500BC.

Celts and Scholars

We have a fuller picture of the Irish from the time of the Celts, wanderers from Europe who came to Ireland in the 6th century BC, although some scholars now say they arrived as far back as the 9th. Historians describe them as individualistic peoples who belonged to loosely knit communities with little political cohesion. Under Celtic rule, Ireland was divided into some 150 kingdoms, which gradually began to cement into larger groupings under the High Kings of Ulster, Connacht, Munster and Leinster.

After the fall of the Roman Empire, scholarly monks retreated westwards from those parts of northern Europe most ravaged by opportunistic invaders. In the 5th century, many sought sanctuary in Ireland and kept Christian civilisation alive with their building, writing and teaching skills. Old pagan sites served as foundations for the new religion and for the construction of monastic settlements. There is evidence of harmony between Christian myth and the earlier Celtic pantheon of demi-gods, half-mortals and wizards, whose ancient lore was written down rather than condemned. These manuscripts of myths and legends are a valuable part of the nation's literary heritage. The most renowned is the mythological saga of *Táin Bó Cuailnge*, which now resides alongside the famous illuminated manuscript of the New Testament, known as the *Book of Kells*, in Trinity College Library, Dublin.

By the 7th and 8th centuries, Irish monasteries were renowned throughout Christendom for their Latin learning, writing and art. Pupils came to Ireland from the Continent, and staunch missionaries went out from Ireland with their teachings. This was the time of Ireland's Golden Age, when numerous monasteries were built with their churches, high crosses and round towers (which acted as beacons, bell towers and forts in time of siege). This was also the time

Left: the Arrest of Christ from the *Book of Kells*
Right: Celtic high cross

when priceless art and bejewelled and enamelled artefacts were being made and manuscripts illuminated, like the *Book of Kells* (8th century), the Tara Brooch and the Ardagh Chalice (the former is now in Trinity College; the latter two are in the National Museum, Dublin).

By the end of the 8th century, the now-thriving monasteries attracted pillaging and plundering from the Vikings, who established their settle-

ments along Ireland's coast and founded ports such as Dublin, Wexford and Cork. Constant warfare between the invaders and the Celts finally resulted in the defeat of the Vikings by Brian Ború in 1014 at the Battle of Clontarf. Even so, Brian Ború, the most celebrated of Ireland's High Kings, died in the battle, and with his passing the old Gaelic order changed. For a century more, battles and turmoil prevailed until one king sought an alliance with the Normans in Wales, who only a hundred years before had invaded and subdued England successfully.

With the arrival of the Norman invaders led by Strongbow in 1169, came a new order: towns, ports, roads, laws and feudalism were established. The Normans suppressed the Celtic heritage but, being of the same faith, they vigorously set about building bigger and better cathedrals, churches, abbeys, friaries and priories. Many of these still survive around Ireland: from the grandiose religious complexes of Kilkenny and Kells to simple Romanesque churches. Likewise castles mushroomed; the square Norman towers that we spy strewn across the landscape today were built, ravaged and rebuilt between the 13th and the 17th centuries.

The result of all this building is a palimpsest of history. As we travel round Ireland, it is not unusual to see a modern family home built against a broken castle of the 15th century, adjacent to a ruined monastic site of the 10th century with a 4,000-year-old cairn nearby. The events of ensuing centuries have left less of a mark on the landscape and impinge upon us little as we travel through the country, but they have left an indelible memory in the hearts and minds of the Irish people.

English Rule

With the Norman invasion, Ireland effectively came under the control of the English monarchs. Initially the incoming Normans intermarried, built their castles and extended their own influence to become powerful barons and landowners. It would not be long before an English monarch sought to exercise authority over these powerful and independent barons. In the 15th century, Henry VIII demanded that all Irish lands be surrendered to him. Those who accepted Henry's dictum had their lands 'regranted by the grace of the King'. Those who refused had their lands taken away and given to the 'planters', loyal Protestant supporters of the king, many of whom came from England and Scotland.

Above: two-faced pre-Christian stone figure
Right: Powerscourt Estate, County Wicklow

The arrival of the planters sowed the seeds of the inter-religious strife that still divides Ulster today. Subsequently English monarchs pursued a policy of suppressing the Irish Catholics, and Oliver Cromwell was one of the most ruthless of all: Irish rebellions were bloodily crushed by Cromwell's army between 1649 and 1652, after which most Irish lands that still remained in Catholic hands were granted to the Protestants. Matters came to a head in 1690 when the deposed Catholic King, James II of England, was defeated by William of Orange at the Battle of the Boyne, which took place near Dublin *(see Itinerary 2, page 28)*. The following year, under the terms of the Treaty of Limerick, some 14,000 Irish soldiers and landowners were forced into exile, an event known ever since as the 'Flight of the Wild Geese'.

Ireland was left bereft of its young men and its leaders; new laws ensured that Catholics could only lease land for a maximum of 31 years. Resentment against absentee English landlords fanned the smouldering embers of Irish nationalism, but the road to independence was long, slow and bloody.

Despite the inequity and strife of the 18th century, it was a time of great building in Ireland, when the Georgian edifices that grace the centres of so many Irish cities were constructed. In Dublin, major public buildings rose on the banks of the River Liffey – the Bank of Ireland building (then the Irish Parliament), Leinster House and the Four Courts. With them came wide streets, crescents, squares and parks; mansions and terraced town houses. In the countryside palatial private residences, such as Russborough, Powerscourt, Castletown, Bantry and Newbridge House, to name but a few, were also being built by master architects.

The Road to Independence

On the political front, the road to independence was marked by steps forward then backward. The Great Rebellion of 1798 against English rule, led by Wolfe Tone, was crushed with the loss of 50,000 lives. In 1800 the Irish parliament was dissolved and, under the Act of Union, Ireland became part of the United Kingdom, but without Catholic representation in the House of Commons; that did not come until 1829, with the passing of the Catholic Emancipation Act.

In 1845, potato blight destroyed crops of Ireland's staple food. The Great Famine hit the rural peasant hardest. It is said that a million people died of starvation and another million – driven off the land they could not afford to rent – emigrated to America. American Irish were later to provide the funds that supported the rising Republican movement, committed to achieving independence, even by armed struggle if necessary. Others sought effective but peaceful means to ensure that the Irish could own and farm their land. Charles Stewart Parnell set up the National Land League; supporters of the League agreed not to rent land from which the previous tenant had been evicted. Captain Boycott, who took over an estate in County Mayo, was so effectively ostracised by his neighbours that his name entered the language.

Parnell's objectives were relatively modest in that he sought 'Home Rule' for Ireland, rather than absolute independence. Ireland itself was divided and, whilst huge numbers of Irish volunteers were fighting for the British army on the Western Front during World War I, others joined the vigilante Irish Volunteers and staged the Easter Rising of 24 April 1916. The Volunteers occupied Dublin's General Post Office building for about a week before the British defeated them; most of the leaders were executed and many of the participants were interned. Before the executions, many Dubliners were indifferent to the rebels' cause; after them, they became violently anti-British.

Between 1919 and 1921, Britain and Ireland were effectively at war, with the Irish Republican Army pitted against British police and troops in an escalating spiral of violence and revenge killings. In October 1921, British and Irish representatives sat down in

Above: O'Connell Street during the Easter Rising, 1916
Right: statue of Parnell, O'Connell Street, Dublin

London to thrash out a settlement and the official independence document was finally signed on 5 December. The stumbling block had been resistance from the north-east, where the dominant Protestant population was prepared to take up arms to resist a united Ireland. The compromise was partition, with six of Ulster's nine counties remaining within Britain as Northern Ireland, with their own parliament. The issue of whether partition should be accepted resulted in a bitter civil war in the new Free State in 1922–3.

The Republic Today

Today, the Republic of Ireland's two main political parties are the descendants of the civil war opponents: Fine Gael (who accepted partition) and Fianna Fáil (against), although younger parties are gaining increasing influence. The problem of a divided Ireland has not gone away, but the Republic has matured to play an important part in the European Union, and relations between Britain and Ireland – on the non-political level – are close, especially since the UK is Ireland's main trading partner. Since entry to the EC in 1973, Ireland has profited from European subsidies galore. European Structural Funds have been used to build new motorways and cultural centres, and to restore historic buildings, such as those in the Temple Bar quarter of Dublin. In 1994 increasing Irish prosperity meant that the Republic became ineligible for further large-scale subsidies, but the Irish economy continued to perform well, becoming the world's second fastest growing economy. Unemployment figures went on falling in spite of the fact that hundreds of returning emigrants and foreign nationals were entering the country every week.

While all this new prosperity was welcome to a people long inured to the forced emigration of some 30,000 young people every year, the powerful phenomenon that is the 'Celtic tiger' has two sides to its nature. House prices, keeping pace with demand, went through the roof, and rising sales of new cars made Dublin rush-hour traffic even more of a nightmare. To combat this, a light rail system is under construction, along with other remedial measures presently under discussion.

The social exclusion of certain ghetto areas which prevents them from participating in the economic bonanza, has exacerbated a drug problem that, in turn, has caused an increase in crime. Some communities have joined forces to drive the pushers out of their areas, with no small degree of success, but this is a problem with no easy solution. Also, Ireland's comparatively liberal immigration laws have attracted much larger numbers of asylum seekers than in the past, some of whom, sad to say, did not meet with the famous *céad míle fáilte* (one hundred thousand welcomes).

Social changes in the 1990s included the introduction of divorce by referendum, the loosening of laws on abortion and the election of the first woman president, Mary Robinson. The more open atmosphere also inevitably

Above: Dublin suffers from chronic traffic congestion

brought to light evidence of corruption in high places, such as sexual abuse scandals involving the clergy and allegations of malpractice involving financial institutions, public officials and even government ministers. Most notable was the case of ex-Taoiseach Charles Haughey, accused of receiving vast sums of money for his personal use from a Dublin businessman.

Events in Northern Ireland, torn by violence and terrorism since 1969, continued to inspire hope and despair. On 10 April 1998, the parties involved in the Stormont peace talks signed the historic 'Good Friday Agreement'. After a referendum, north and south of the border, showed overwhelming support for the agreement, the Irish government changed the constitution by deleting its territorial claim to the six counties of Northern Ireland. However, the Unionists refused to participate in any governing body until the IRA began handing over its weapons, and it wasn't until late 1999 that an all-party assembly was set up to provide demonstrably fair government. Various political crises have caused it to be suspended from time to time, with temporary reimposition of direct rule from London, but the fragile peace holds, allowing for a slow progress towards stability in the North.

Looking to the Future

The global economic slowdown that began in 2001 finally reined in the Celtic tiger, and the Republic's adoption of the euro in 2002 restricted the short-term options for tweaking the economy. Whatever the economic prospects, though, the Irish have always known how to enjoy themselves – tourists come from every corner of the world to experience the *craic* (fun) unique to this country and the Irish continue to export their talent for storytelling and entertainment. U2, Sinéad O'Connor, Enya and the Corrs are among the bigger success stories in music; Irish dancing received a huge boost from the phenomenal success of the show *Riverdance*, and books such as Frank McCourt's *Angela's Ashes* have kept Ireland on the bestseller list.

Such confidence helped inspire the controversial 120-metre (390-ft) Millennium Spire erected on the former site in Dublin's O'Connell Street of Nelson's Pillar, blown up by the IRA in 1966. Ian Ritchie, the architect, said he was providing the capital 'with a symbol that reached for the sky'.

HISTORY HIGHLIGHTS

6,000BC First known traces of man in Ireland.

6th century Celtic migrations to Ireland.

AD432 St Patrick comes to Ireland as a missionary.

500–800 Early monasticism; Ireland becomes a European centre of learning.

9th century Vikings invade and settle.

841 Dublin is founded.

1014 BrianBorú defeats the Vikings and breaks their power.

1169 Norman invasion.

1537 Reformation doctrines promulgated by Henry VIII, who orders the dissolution of the Irish monasteries.

1556 First 'planters' arrive from England and Scotland.

1649–52 The Great Rebellion is crushed by Oliver Cromwell.

1690 Battle of the Boyne.

1691 Treaty of Limerick and exile of the 'Wild Geese'.

1713 Jonathan Swift is appointed Dean of St Patrick's Cathedral in Dublin.

1798 The second 'Great Rebellion', led by Wolfe Tone, is crushed; 50,000 die.

1800 The Act of Union.

1801 Legislative union of Great Britain and Ireland.

1829 Daniel O'Connell ('the Liberator') wins the right for Catholics to enter the British parliament.

1845 Beginning of the Great Famine caused by potato blight.

1858 Irish Republican Brotherhood, forerunner of the IRA, founded.

1875 Charles Stewart Parnell is elected MP for Meath and becomes leader of the Home Rule movement.

1885 Parnell's party holds the balance of power in the House of Commons. Home Rule becomes a major issue but is defeated in the House of Lords.

1912 Protestants under Sir Edward Carson establish an illegal militia – the Ulster Volunteer Force – to oppose Home Rule; the south responds with the Irish National Volunteers.

1916 The Easter Rising rebels are defeated, their leaders executed, and martial law imposed.

1918 The Sinn Féin party gains sweeping victories in the first post-war general election. It boycotts the House of Commons, sets up its own parliament in Ireland and elects the jailed Eamonn de Valera as president.

1919 Guerrilla war between the IRA and British anti-terrorist forces – the 'Black and Tans'.

1921 Britain and Ireland sign a treaty granting Dominion status to most of Ireland. The six counties of Ulster remain part of the UK.

1922–3 Civil war between pro- and anti-partitionists in Ireland

1939–45 Controversially, Ireland remains neutral in World War II.

1949 Ireland becomes a Republic.

1969 'The Troubles', initially a civil rights dispute, erupt in Northern Ireland.

1973 Ireland joins the European Community (now the European Union).

1990 Mary Robinson elected president.

1993–4 Downing Street Agreement starts a new peace dialogue culminating in a temporary IRA ceasefire.

1997 Divorce becomes legal. IRA declares another ceasefire.

1998 Good Friday Agreement. David Trimble and John Hume receive the Nobel Peace Prize.

1999 An all-party assembly with limited powers set up in Northern Ireland.

2002 The Republic adopts the euro. In the North, trust breaks down between Unionists and Nationalists and direct rule from London is reimposed.

2003 Elections in Northern Ireland restore the all-party assembly.

2004 Ireland bans smoking in all workplaces – even pubs.

Left: Ireland has one of the youngest populations in Europe

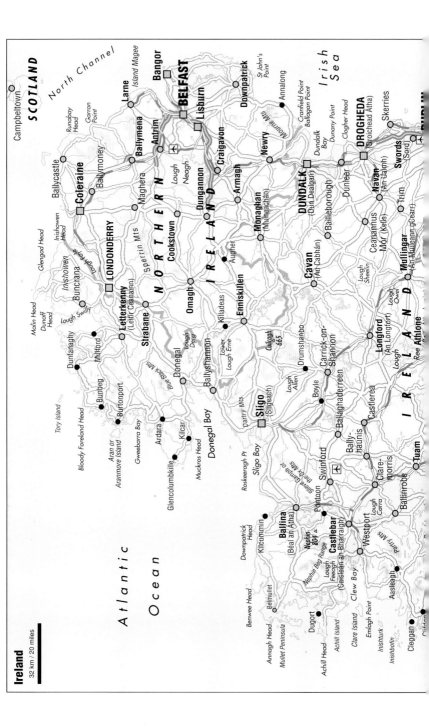

Ireland

32 km / 20 miles

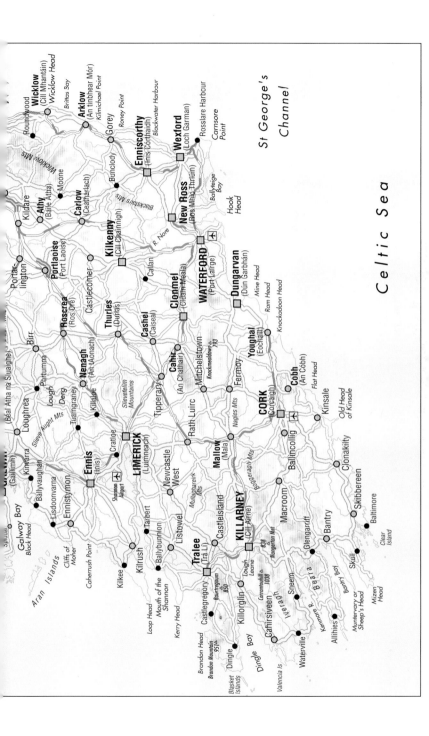

Dublin

The main stronghold of Ireland's invaders, who called it "the Pale", Dublin has absorbed various cultures, from the Vikings to the English, to create its own unique identity. The first three itineraries of this book are based around here, so you can use its mixed character as a stepping stone to immersing yourself in Irish culture literally "beyond the Pale".

The remaining 14 itineraries are organised geographically, starting in Donegal in the north, working southward to Bantry and then eastward from Cork to Wexford. The itineraries assume that you will hire a car and drive around Ireland. If you are a lover of remote scenic beauty, then you will probably find *Itineraries 4–8* of particular interest, whilst cultural interests are better met by *Itineraries 9–17,* which cover the part of Ireland that has most by way of castles, manors, monuments and museums.

Since each of the itineraries lasts a full day, it would be impossible to follow all of them in the course of a short visit. The idea is to choose and combine those itineraries that most interest you. As Ireland is a small country, most areas are accessible from Dublin.

1. A DAY IN DUBLIN *(see map p22)*

Your first day in Ireland is best spent getting to know the capital and the best way to do this is on foot. Dublin is one of Europe's smallest capital cities and almost everything is within walking distance. This leisurely day-long itinerary will show you the major sights: Trinity College Library and the *Book of Kells*; the National Gallery of Ireland; Dublin Castle; Christchurch Cathedral; Dublinia; the Guinness Brewery and Temple Bar.

Leave your car safely locked in the hotel car park for the day (as in all European capitals, finding secure street parking is difficult at the best of times). Entering Trinity College via the gate on College Green you'll see that it's now a popular meeting point. Just inside, Trinity students offer tours of the campus for €10. Follow the signs to the Book of Kells, then cross the courtyard to the **Thomas Davis Theatre** to see the audio-visual presentation, *The Dublin Experience* (May–Sept: 10am–6pm). This will help you orientate yourself and learn some of the city's history.

Founded by Vikings in AD841, the walled town of Dublin hardly grew during the Middle Ages when the principal public buildings

Left: the Ha'penny Bridge near Temple Bar
Right: a Georgian door

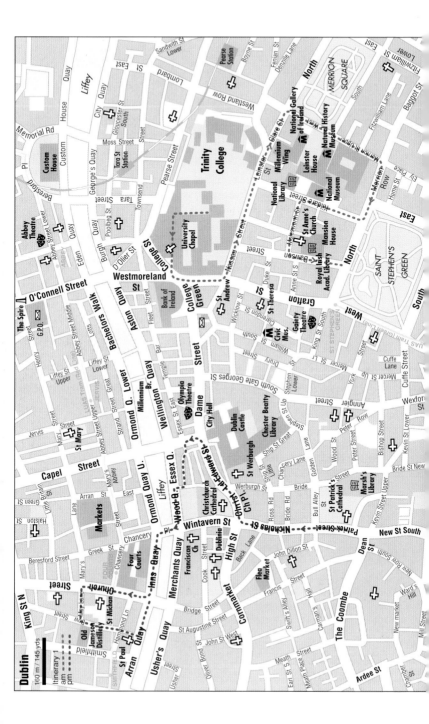

were its castle, of which the Record Tower is original, and Christchurch Cathedral. By the 17th century the city was in virtual decay, but flourished in the 18th century with a sensational building programme to which Dublin's fine looks are attributed. But with the termination of legislative independence from England in 1801, once again decline set in. Driven from the land by famine and land clearances, the displaced came to Dublin and many a fine street descended to slums. Much of the splendid Georgian architecture, seen by some as an unwelcome reminder of colonialism, was allowed to rot or was torn down in the 1960s by property developers; serious restoration attempts are only fairly recent.

Around Trinity College

We will see some of Dublin's Georgian crescents and squares later in the day. For now, having viewed the audio-visual presentation, move on to Trinity College Library's **Long Room, Treasury and Colonnades** (Oct–May Mon–Sat 9.30am–5pm, Sun noon–4.30pm Jun–Sep; Oct–May 12.30–4.30pm), which house some 200,000 books and manuscripts, the highlight being the 8th-century illuminated *Book of Kells* and its accompanying exhibition, 'Darkness Into Light'. Enter via the gift shop. The exhibition introduces the techniques of production and surveys ancient religious history before giving you a view of the books. You then exit via the Long Room. On

leaving the library, go out via the main entrance onto **College Green**. In front is the distinctive **Bank of Ireland** building, built in 1729 to house the Irish parliament but made redundant after parliament voted itself out of existence and authority was transferred to London in 1801. Visitors are welcome to view the old House of Lords room – the only part of the building preserved from its previous function (Mon–Fri 9.30am–4pm; tours Tues).

From here turn around and retrace your steps past the college up Westmoreland Street. On the right-hand side is the statue of **Molly Malone**. Love it or hate it, this busty statue is a great favourite with visitors to the city, many of whom cannot help bursting into a rendition of 'cockles and mussels, alive, alive O!' Tempted as you may be to continue up the pedestrian way of Grafton Street, I recommend going left along **Nassau Street**. This is something of a centre for craft shops, chief among which are Blarney Woollen Mills and the Kilkenny Shop. At the end of Leinster Street, turn right at Merrion Street Upper, just after Green's famous book store, well worth a browse.

Across the road is **Merrion Square**, one of Dublin's finest addresses.

The first turn on the right takes us up to the **National Gallery of Ireland** (Mon–Sat 9.30am–5.30pm; Thur 9.30am–8.30pm; Sun noon–5.30pm). It

Above: the Long Room, in Trinity College
Left: statue of Molly Malone

is worth a visit to see the Rembrandts, a recently discovered Caravaggio and the 'Amorino' or Cupid, a recently acquired masterpiece by Canova. There is also a distinguished Anglo-Irish collection, and an entire room has been devoted to the works of Jack B Yeats and his family. The new Millennium Wing provides space for international touring exhibitions. Fitzer's restaurant inside is a great place for coffee or an early lunch.

Continuing up Merrion Street brings you to the **Natural History Museum**, which has an extensive collection. Despite its local nickname – the 'Dead Zoo' – the museum houses a weird yet endearing collection. Further along on the right are the guarded gates of government buildings that contain the office of the *Taoiseach* (or head of government) and the Cabinet Room. Guided tours are available – get your tickets in the National Gallery (Sat 10am–2.15pm). Next, turn right on Merrion Row, getting your first glimpse of the magnificent buildings around St Stephen's Green. Just past the Shelbourne Hotel, where the Constitution was drawn up, is Kildare Street, into which you turn. The **National Museum** (Tues–Sat 10am–5pm; Sun 2–5pm; free) is well worth a visit for its unique archaeological collection. Amongst these are the superbly crafted Ardagh Chalice, Cross of Cong and Tara Brooch, plus Europe's finest collection of prehistoric gold artefacts.

Next door is the main entrance to Leinster House, built in 1745. Now the seat of the Irish Parliament, it can be viewed when the house is not in session. Cross over the road, turn left along Molesworth Street (full of private art galleries) and left again up Dawson Street. Immediately on the left is **St Anne's Church**, noted for its occasional lunchtime recitals (Mon–Fri 10am–4pm). After this, pass the **Royal Irish Academy Library** with its collection of manuscripts (Mon–Thur 10am–5.30pm, Fri until 5pm), then the Lord Mayor's residence, known as the **Mansion House** (built 1710) now the location of Fado, a modern, fine-dining restaurant (Tel: 676 7200).

St Stephen's Green

Facing you is **St Stephen's Green**, one of Europe's largest squares. The Green, a common until 1664, became an elegant spot by Georgian times, lined with gracious 18th-century mansions, many of which remain. The

square's neat flowerbeds and ponds were financed by the Guinness brewing dynasty in the 1880s. Free lunchtime recitals are held in summer.

In fact, now is a good time to think of lunch. The Green has several restaurants, from the formality of the Shelbourne Hotel dining rooms to the elegance of the Commons Restaurant in **Newman House** (85 St Stephen's Green). This erstwhile seat of University College Dublin, once two townhouses, has the city's finest Georgian interior, with superb plasterwork and some marvellous baroque detail. The building can be viewed by guided tour only. Another option is to head back up to Grafton Street where a near limitless supply of street cafes line its many tributaries.

Cathedrals and Castles

After lunch, take a taxi to **St Patrick's Cathedral** (daily 9am–6pm except Nov–Feb Sat 9am–5pm and Sun 9am–3pm). This is believed to have been founded on the site where St Patrick baptised converts. There are many monuments here to ponder over, including the bust and epitaph of Jonathan Swift (author of *Gulliver's Travels*), who was dean here for 30 years. Look out, too, for the Chapter House door. The expression 'chancing your arm' was derived from a feud that ended with a handshake through the hole in this door.

From here, head towards the River Liffey, along Patrick Street, to **Christchurch Cathedral** (10am–5pm except for services); this was founded in 1038, although the current structure dates back to the late 12th century, as the cathedral took over a century and a half to build. If you have the energy, first visit **Dublinia** (summer 10am–5pm; winter Mon–Sat 11am–4pm, Sun 10am–4.30pm), set in Synod Hall, next door to the cathedral. This multimedia exhibition presents a medieval fayre where, among other things, you can do a brass rubbing of yourself as mayor of Dublin, or discover an ancient cure for what ails you. A bridge links the exhibition with the cathedral, and a tour of the building is included in the entrance fee. Don't miss the treasures on display in the crypt, or the effigy of a recumbent knight with a small figure lying alongside. Legend has it that this is the **tomb of Strongbow**, the knight who conquered Ireland for the Normans. Some say the smaller figure is Eva, his wife, and others that it is Strongbow's son, supposedly executed by him for fleeing the battlefield.

Turning from such gruesome thoughts, walk down Lord Edward Street to **Dublin Castle** (Mon–Fri 10am–5pm; Sat–Sun 2–5pm). The castle dates from 1204, but only the Record Tower survives from Norman times. Acting as the administrative centre of English power, the castle was subject to attack and was badly damaged by a fire in 1684 and the events of the 1916 Easter Rising. The present castle is a palatial affair but it is worth visiting the grim undercroft, which contains elements of the original Viking and Norman strongholds. The main feature is a lavish set of State Apartments, surrounding a magnificent courtyard, designed as ceremonial quarters for the English Viceroys who once ruled Ireland. Also worth noting is the statuary on the walls – 90 carved heads of British monarchs and bishops. Behind the castle the **Chester Beatty Library**

Left: St Patrick's Cathedral
Right: detail from Dublin Castle

(Oct–Apr, Tues–Fri 10am–5pm; May–Sep, Mon–Fri 10am–5pm; Sat 11am–5pm; Sun 1–5pm) houses a marvellous collection of Oriental manuscripts and paintings. From the castle, go down to **Wood Quay**, on the banks of the Liffey; it was here that the Vikings founded the first city of Dublin in the 9th century. Office blocks now stand over the site where Viking remains were found.

Cross the Liffey to reach the **Four Courts** (Mon–Fri 11am–1pm, 2–4pm). This classical building, dominating the Northern Quays, was completed in

1802 and houses the Irish Law Courts. It was partly destroyed in the 1922 Civil War, but its restoration has been much admired. The dominant lantern dome is fronted by a six-columned Corinthian portico surmounted by the statues of Moses, Justice and Mercy.

Leaving the Four Courts, turn right on Church Street to visit the church of **St Michan** (Mon–Fri 10am–12.45pm, 2–4.45pm; Sat 10am–12.45pm) dating from the 17th century. The organ, upon which Handel is said to have played, features some excellent wood carvings. The church's other major curiosity is the vault where bodies have lain for centuries without decomposing and are now mummified. From here a left turn into May Lane brings you to the **Old Jameson Distillery** (daily 9.30am–5pm) where you can learn about the art of making Irish whiskey and, of course, taste the end product. Afterwards, take the lift to the top of the **Smithfield Chimney** (daily all year) for a bird's-eye view of the city.

By now you have earned a rest, so take a taxi back to the elegant bars of the Shelbourne Hotel. Alternatively, if you are feeling energetic, explore Dublin's bohemian 'Left Bank', called **Temple Bar**. To get there, return to Dublin Castle and take any turning left off Dame Street between the castle and the front of Trinity College. Plan your evening while drinking a Guinness in the Art Deco downstairs bar of the Clarence Hotel (Wellington Quay), owned by the rock band U2. This is the heart of Temple Bar, once a low-life quarter of disused warehouses but now revived as a vibrant maze of trendy bars and restaurants. Some find it overpriced and overcrowded, so you may settle instead for a literary pub crawl. One starts at 7.30pm nightly in summer at the Duke (Duke Street, off Grafton Street; tel: 679 9553 for information).

If you are so enamoured of Dublin's charm that you want to spend another day in the city, I suggest you spend it shopping (see *Shopping, page 69*) and consider a visit to the **Guinness Brewery** (James St) whence the dark stout has been flowing for 250 years. Beside the brewery is the **Guinness Storehouse**, housing archives, exhibition areas and an all-new 'visitor experience' including a tasting in the highest bar in Dublin (daily all year 9.30am–5pm; until 9pm July–Aug; tel: 453 8364).

Above: nightlife in Dublin's Temple Bar

2. THE BOYNE VALLEY *(see map below)*

A circular day-trip taking you north of Dublin to the Boyne Valley, where 5,000 years of history are encapsulated in the megalithic grave at Newgrange, the Hill of Slane where Christianity was brought to Ireland by St Patrick, aristocratic houses and the site of the Battle of the Boyne.

From Dublin city follow the airport signs, which will take you northward on the N1. Passing by the airport, continue on to Swords, where you turn right to Malahide on the R106, following the signs to **Malahide Castle** (Apr–Oct, Mon–Fri 10am–5pm, Sat and Sun 11am–6pm; Nov–Mar, Mon–Fri 10am–5pm, Sat and Sun 2–5pm; no tours between 12.45–2pm). Founded in Norman times, it was the seat of the Talbot family for 800 years. The castle is now owned by Dublin City, and houses the National Gallery's portrait collection, Ireland's largest. Today the medieval Great Hall is used for state banquets. The outbuildings house the **Fry Model Railway Museum** (Apr–Sept, Mon–Sat 10am–5pm, closed 1–2pm; Sun 2–6pm), a working miniature impression of Ireland's rail system.

Retrace your route back along the R106 and turn right before Swords to continue north on the N1. About 5km (3 miles) on, turn right on the R127 to **Lusk**. St MacCuilinn, who died in 497, is buried in a cave here, though nobody is quite sure where. Most noticeable is the unusual conglomeration of an 11th-century round tower, a medieval belfry and a 19th-century church, which now houses the Lusk Heritage Centre (mid-Jun–mid-Sept Fri only 10am–5pm; tours on request).

Back on the R127, a quiet road across gentle farmlands, take a left turn following the sign for **Ardgillan Demesne**, a charming 1738 castle that houses an exhibition of maps, including the 17th-century *Down Survey of Ireland*. The magnificent parkland has unrivalled views of the coastline.

Return to the R127 and continue to Skerries, said to be the spot where St Patrick landed to convert the Irish to Christianity in the 5th century. Drive on along the coast through Balbriggan, a fishing village, and take the N1 to **Drogheda**. This historic seaport began with the Vikings, became a Norman

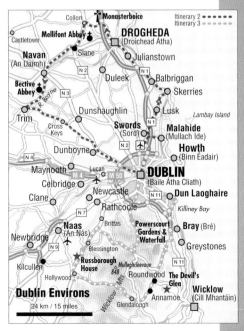

Above: Malahide Castle

stronghold in the 12th century and truly flourished in the 15th century. In 1649 Cromwell's army committed an atrocious massacre here, burning defenders and civilians alive in St Peter's Church. The church is also famous for St Oliver Plunkett, executed in 1681, whose head lies embalmed on the far side of the altar. The town has many beautiful buildings. You can obtain details of walking

tours from the tourist centre. If you are here around lunchtime, you will not be disappointed by the **Boyne Restaurant** at the Boyne Valley Hotel (Stameen, Drogheda; tel: 041-9837737).

Some 6km (3¾ miles) beyond Drogheda on the N1 you see the signs for **Monasterboice**, one of Ireland's exceptional monastic sites, dating from the rather obscure St Buite, who died in 521. The monastery fell into disuse in the 12th century and only ruins remain, except for the most excellent Round Tower and three high crosses.

Continue past the ruins until you reach the R68 and see signs pointing to the Cistercian site of **Mellifont Abbey**, which finally fell into disuse in the 18th century. In the 13th century this was the ecclesiastical centre for 35 other monasteries in the district. Of special interest is the octagonal *lavabo* (wash-room), with its Romanesque features (May–Oct, daily 10am–6pm).

Continue southwest to the rather muddy-looking River Boyne, with pleasant deciduous woods and fields along its banks, to the **battle site**. It was here, in 1690, that the forces of the Protestant William of Orange defeated the Catholic King James II, and lost him his claim to the British throne, thus transforming English, French and Irish history. The battlefield is signposted with a viewing point and an explanation of manoeuvres and tactics used by both sides during the struggle (guided tours May–Sep 10am–6pm; tel: 041-982 6459).

Newgrange and Slane

Follow the signs to sensational **Newgrange** (9.30am–5pm or 7pm, depending on daylight). Accessed through the Brú na Bóinne Visitor Centre, this massive 5,000-year-old passage grave, with its glistening white quartz walls surrounding 200,000 tons of rock, has been thoroughly excavated. A similar tomb at **Knowth** can be viewed (May–Oct: same times as above); another at **Dowth** is still being worked over. Newgrange tomb is rated one of the most spectacular archaeological sites in Europe and is extremely popular, so arrive early. The excellent guided tour takes you 19m (62ft) into its central chamber, decorated with Neolithic ring markings. The highlight is the well-presented re-enactment of the tomb's astronomical significance; light floods the chamber to represent the beam of sunlight that penetrates the core for 20 minutes at the winter solstice. Emerging from the tomb, one hardly notices that the hillside, hidden from view by hedges, has hundreds of humps, tumps and megaliths, indicating how impressive the area must have been around 3000BC.

Above: St Muiredach Cross
Right: visitors at Newgrange

dublin

Your next move takes you a short distance along a narrow lane to the neat and charming manorial village of **Slane**. At the west end is the beautifully restored castle seat of the Mountcharles family, now a venue for pop concerts (guided tours May–Sep, closed mid-Aug). The village is better known as the home of the soldier poet Francis Ledgwig. One kilometre (½ mile) north, on the N2, is the **Hill of Slane** where St Patrick lit a great bonfire for Christianity in AD433. The site has interesting ecclesiastical ruins associated with St Earc. If you have not yet had lunch, the **Conygham Arms Hotel** (tel: 041-9824155) in the centre of Slane offers a hearty self-service buffet.

Leaving Slane in a westerly direction, your route takes you to Navan on the N51, the county town of Meath, centre for furniture making and nearby lead and zinc mines. Your main target is Bective Abbey, 8km (5 miles) beyond on the R161 Trim road. Before this, though, turn off for the **Hill of Tara**, the ancient seat of the High Kings of Ireland. An audiovisual presentation and guided tour add flesh to the legend (May–Oct, daily 10am–6pm).

The 12th-century **Bective Abbey** has more to offer, though the sense of legend might be less powerful. This delightful ruin contains the body of Hugh de Lacy, who died in 1195, minus his head which was interred in Dublin. A 10-year dispute arose when the monks sought the return of the head, resulting in a ruling from the Pope in Avignon.

A further 8km (5 miles) takes us to **Trim**, dominated by its 12th-century D-shaped castle, regarded as a classic example of its type since it has undergone very little alteration since the day it was built. The town also offers an intriguing group of medieval monuments including the Yellow Steeple, built on the site of an Augustinian abbey that once housed a fabled statue of Our Lady, destroyed during the Reformation. Some 2km (1¼ miles) further on is the long church of Saints Peter and Paul; the refectory building creates a curious echo if you yell at it from the friary of St John the Baptist, across the river. Trim's visitor centre has information on these monuments. From here, Dublin is 38km (23½ miles) southeast along the R154 and N3.

3. Scenic County Wicklow *(see map p27)*

A day-long drive south from Dublin following the coast to the James Joyce Tower, through wooded countryside to Powerscourt House with its ornate gardens, on to the historic ecclesiastical site of Glendalough; then Russborough House with its art treasures, before crossing the mountains at Sally Gap and returning to Dublin.

Drive south from Dublin along Merrion Road or Beach Street following the signs for Blackrock or Dun Laoghaire. At Sandycove is the **Joyce Museum** in the old Martello tower that features in the opening scene of *Ulysses* (Apr–Oct Mon–Sat 10am–1pm and 2–5pm; Sun 2–6pm). Joyce memorabilia is displayed, including manuscripts and musical instruments. Below the tower is the Forty Foot, a deep bathing pool.

Beyond lies the Sorrento Road following the cliff top; this flows into Vico Road, with its noble views of Killiney Bay and Dalkey Island. At the railway station turn right up Military Road, away from the coast, then left (south) on the N11. Turn right when you see the sign for **Powerscourt** (summer, daily 9.30am–5.30pm; winter 9.30am to dusk). Designed by Richard Cassells in the 1740s, this palladian mansion was gutted by fire in 1974 and only re-opened again in 1997. It has been refurbished and re-glazed, with the interior converted to house a terrace café, visitor centre and several shops. The formal gardens – embellished with statues, wrought-iron work, and pebble-mosaic terraces – are fabled throughout Europe for their layout and setting. In addition there are Italian, Japanese and walled gardens, plus herbaceous borders and greenhouses. Within the estate is the **Powerscourt Waterfall** (summer, daily 9.30am–dusk; winter 10.30am to dusk) with a 90-m (300-ft) silvery ribbon of water tumbling into a wooded glen, an ideal area for walks and picnics, but too busy in high summer for real peace and quiet. Children will enjoy the new playground.

Glendalough

Ahead lies **Glendalough** – the valley with the two lakes. Follow the signs along the R755. The Glendalough Hotel (tel: 0404-45135) is usually packed

to the rafters, so unless you've booked ahead it would probably be better to stop in Laragh (about 2km/1 mile before Glendalough) for a bite to eat. It is ironic that St Kevin, who turned his back on the good life to become a recluse, and who founded this enormous monastic settlement around AD570, should now be the top-of-the-tourist-pops.

Glendalough is best explored by starting at the visitor centre (Nov–Mar 9.30am– 5pm; Mar–Oct 9am–6pm) to see the audio-visual presentation and enjoy the brilliant exhibition about Ireland's early ecclesiastical sites. The **Cathedral**, a Romanesque church containing early Christian gravestones, is open to all, but **St Kevin's Kitchen**, the oddly named tiny church topped by a small round tower is only accessible on guided tours, which leave from the visitor's centre. There is a great sense of serenity here when there are few visitors, encouraging you to take your time wandering amongst the sites, which are scattered over a 2½km (1½ mile) stretch of the valley.

Russborough House and the Sally Gap

From Glendalough continue west on the R756 to Hollywood. The idea is to turn right to Russborough House, but if you are addicted to stone circles turn left for the **Piper Stones**, so called because legend has it that this is where the fairies gather to play the uilleann (Irish) bagpipes. After visiting the stones, turn round and drive northward up the N81, turning left at the sign for **Russborough House** (10am–5pm daily May–Sept; Sun only in Apr and Oct). This Palladian mansion was built in the 1740s for the Earl of Milltown. Although it has suffered from IRA-linked thefts of its art collection, Russborough is the most lavishly furnished mansion in the southeast. The grandest room is the saloon, with its feast of rococo plasterwork, attributed to the Lafranchini brothers.

From here drive on to Blessington via the N81 and continue beside man-made Blessington Lakes before turning right for the **Sally Gap** a few kilometres beyond. This begins a scenic drive along the ridges of the Wicklow Mountains, with hardly a building in sight. At the Sally Gap turn left; there is no sign but this is the direction for Dublin. Here we are close to the source of the River Liffey. You will notice the peat cutting areas in this upland bog to which Dubliners have ancient rights. Simply follow the road, which descends in to the city.

Left: the Wicklow Mountains
Above: St Kevin's Kitchen. **Right:** exploring the countryside by bike

The Northwest

4. DONEGAL TO SLIGO *(see map below)*

You can drive from Donegal town to Sligo in an hour, but this tour takes all day, beginning with a look at Donegal town, then taking in Lough Eske, the Creevykeel Court Cairn and, perhaps, a boat ride out to Innishmurray, before visiting Lissadell House and Drumcliffe, with its high cross and the churchyard where W.B. Yeats lies. On this drive you are never more than 5 minutes from golden beaches, so if the weather is good, plan for a swim and sunbathing.

Donegal town was founded by the Vikings at the point where the Eske River meets the sea. In this delightful town's central square, known as the 'Diamond', an obelisk celebrates Brother Michael O'Cleary's classic history of Ireland, the *Annals of the Four Masters*. Finished in 1636, it is today considered a literary masterpiece.

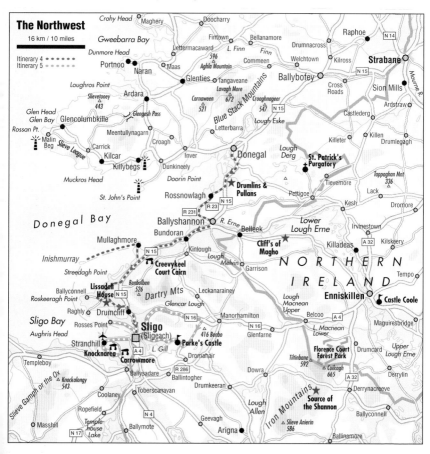

The Northwest

16 km / 10 miles

Itinerary 4 ••••••
Itinerary 5 ••••••

Donegal Castle, a 15th-century restored Norman tower house beside the swift-running Eske, was once the seat of the O'Donnells. The last of this ancient clan, Red Hugh O'Donnell, was forced into exile in Spain after his defeat at Kinsale in 1601. The Jacobean manor house is attributed to Sir Basil Brooke, a planter, who transformed it into a residence in 1611 after the banishment of the last chief. Both sites are open daily Mar–Oct 10am–6pm. Beside the estuary lie the remains of **Donegal Abbey** (built 1474), wrecked by a tremendous explosion during a military siege in 1601.

The town's most famous shop is the Magee department store (located on the Diamond), which stocks a range of handwoven tweeds. As well as selling ready-made clothing, Magee's has a working handloom, an exact replica of those still used in over a hundred Donegal homes to produce tweeds for this long-established company. Just 6km (3½ miles) north of the town is Lough Eske, backed by the Blue Stack Mountains.

Before setting off south, you can take a delightful drive around the lake. This lasts just under an hour. For lunch, return to Donegal for St Ernan's House or the Central Hotel. Waterbus tours of Donegal Bay depart daily from the harbour in summer. The **Donegal Railway Heritage Centre** is situated in the Old Station House (tel: 074 972 2655 for opening times). Leave Donegal by the Sligo road, the N15. A kilometre out is the **Donegal Craft Village** with shops and studios that make and sell pottery, ceramics, textiles, metalwork and jewellery.

Near Benbulben

Some 12km (7½ miles) further on, turn right to Rossnowlagh to take the R231, a more scenic route to **Ballyshannon**, with its magnificent 4km (2½ miles) of sandy beach. The ruins of Kilbarron Castle are at the southern end, whilst Ballyshannon itself is dominated by a modern friary housing **The Abbey Water Wheels Visitor's Centre** with audio-visual display and historical museum.

Above: sheep shearers, County Donegal

At the **Donegal Parian China Factory**, just outside the town on the N15, you can tour the workshops (all year, Mon–Fri 9am–5.30pm, weekends also in summer). Leaving Ballyshannon, move on, looking across Donegal Bay with the might of the Slieve League in the far distance. Pass through Bundoran, a spreading seaside resort, and turn left after 8km (5 miles) to the **Creevykeel Court Cairn**, one of the most extensive in Ireland. Finds from the 1935 Harvard University dig date the tomb to around 2500BC. It is believed that the unroofed courts at the entrances were used by worshippers or mourners.

On the opposite side of the N15 take the R279, a 5-km (3-mile) detour to **Mullaghmore** to see the harbour sandy beach. Weather permitting, you can take a boat to **Innishmurray Island** 7km (4¼ miles) off the Sligo coast. This well-preserved monastic site is surrounded by a defensive stone wall. Inside is a collection of churches, beehive huts, cross-decorated slabs and cursing stones, relics of Ireland's pagan past.

Back on the N15 turn south to Grange and you will start to feel the enchantment of **Benbulben**, the mountain that dominates the landscape on your left. If you are in no hurry, I do advise turning right and following the coastal roads, many of which are so little used that grass grows down the middle; the beaches beckon and there is the unique feeling of travelling between the masses of Benbulben and the Slieve League out across the water.

Near Raghly you may want to look for signs for **Lissadell House**. It was once the home of Constance Gore-Booth, Countess Markievicz, a freedom fighter and the first woman ever elected to Britain's House of Commons. It has fallen into disrepair, but it was purchased by the Cassidy family in 2003 and there are plans to improve the estate and open it to tourists.

Yeats's Grave

From Lissadell it is 5km (3 miles) to **Drumcliffe**, notable for the stump of an early Christian round tower, which was reduced by lightning to its present height in 1396. Legend says the rest will fall down when the wisest man on earth passes beneath. Opposite, in the churchyard amongst the trees, is the **grave of WB Yeats**. Beside the small car park is a fine sculptured high cross, carved with Old Testament scenes dating from the 10th century – all that remains of a monastery founded by St Colmcille in AD575. The grave of the Nobel Prize-winning poet lies to the left of the church. On the stone are inscribed the unsettling words: 'Cast a cold Eye / on Life, on Death. / Horseman, pass by!'

It was Yeats's wish to lie beneath Benbulben and the inscription is the coda of his epitaph: 'Under bare Ben Bulben's head, In Drumcliffe Churchyard

Yeats is laid'. The poet died in France in 1939, leaving behind a body of work that is Irish literature at its finest. His remains were thrown into a French paupers' grave. How much of his body was interred here in 1948 is a moot point, but even if only a bone, Benbulben guards Yeats's dream. Sligo is 8km (5 miles) south along the N15.

5. AROUND SLIGO – YEATS COUNTRY *(see map p32)*

This day-long itinerary begins with a look at Sligo town, followed by a tour around two loughs, Glencar and Gill, before visiting Parkes Castle and the Lake Isle of Innisfree immortalised by Yeats, and the sculpture fantasy trail of Hazelwood. It finishes with a visit to the Carrowmore megalithic graves and the tomb of Queen Maeve at Knocknarea.

Your day begins in **Sligo** itself, a town ravaged and burned in the 1641 rebellion, though the silver bell from the ancient abbey was saved by being stealthily hauled off and deposited beneath the waters of Lough Gill. They say only the pure of heart can hear its peal from the bottom of the lake. The **Dominican Abbey** ruins, dating from the 13th century, are well preserved and are the only vestige of the medieval town remaining. Access is through the visitor centre (Apr–Oct, daily 10am–6pm). The **museum** on Stephen Street (Jun–Sept, Tues–Sat 10am–noon, 2–4.50pm; Oct–May pm only) has interesting exhibits including objects of local interest, plus the manuscripts, memorabilia, Nobel medal and letters of William Butler Yeats. A 10-minute walk away, in The Mall, the Model Arts and Niland Gallery houses a permanent exhibition of the works of Jack B Yeats.

Your journey begins with a diversion of 8km (5 miles) out to **Rosses Point** where the Yeats brothers used to spend their summers at Elsinore Lodge. Today Rosses Point is a typical seaside village with a small pier for boat trips set between the two superb beaches. Returning to Sligo, take the northeasterly N16. Some 14km (8¾ miles) on, turn left at a signpost that says 'Waterfall'. This takes you along the shores of **Glencar Lough** in the Dartry Mountains, a beautiful drive. At the eastern end are two fine waterfalls, one of which drops some 20m (65ft). Nearby is the Swiss Valley, a spectacular wooded ravine. By working your way to the right after Glencar Lough, you can return to the N16 and continue on until you reach the right-hand turn, the R286, which takes you to **Parkes Castle** (mid-Mar–Oct, 10am–6pm daily), set on the shore of Lough Gill. This spectacular lake, 8km (5 miles) long, contains a number of islands, including **Innisfree** where you can reflect on Yeats's words and attain a 'peace that comes dropping slow'.

Parkes Castle has been restored using old building methods. Its current look of a fortified manor house is owed to a planter, Captain Parke, who was awarded the estate after it was confiscated from the O'Rourke family. From here, continue west on the R286 along the shores of Lough Gill to **Hazelwood**, where a forest trail

Right: statue of Yeats in Stephen Street, Sligo

holds some surprises. Dotted along the paths are wooden sculptures ranging from legendary figures and charioteers to some astonishing Art Nouveau concepts (some of which, regrettably, have been vandalised). To the right, a 10-minute walk up the hillside is the **Deerpark megalithic complex**, which has a court souterrain and tomb surrounded by a stone cashel (early fort).

Near Benbulben

Before your next archaeological expedition, it might be a good idea to return to Sligo town, on the R286, for some lunch. For a filling and inexpensive meal, try Beezie's Bar (tel: 07191 45030) in Tobergal Lane.

After lunch, turn right at John Street. Some 3km (1½ miles) later turn left and the grounds of **Carrowmore** begin to appear. The first sight is a particularly fine dolmen in a field on the left. The visitor centre is 1km (½ mile) or so further on, located in some restored cottages. This is the largest cemetery of megalithic tombs in Ireland, and arguably in western Europe. Following recent excavations, it has been estimated that the oldest tombs pre-date Newgrange by almost 1,000 years. Also discovered was shocking new evidence of the practice of scalping in Celtic times. In the 19th century there were 150 Neolithic graves here. In spite of local quarrying in the past century, over 60 structures remain in various stages of preservation, including dolmens, stone circles and passage graves.

On your journey from Sligo, your curiosity may have been aroused by the large mountain to the west, which has a sizeable mound upon its summit. **Knocknarea** is capped by a vast cairn, similar in size and style to Newgrange *(see Itinerary 2, page 28)*. This is reputed to be the tomb of **Queen Maeve** of Connacht, who lived in the 1st century AD, though it actually contains the remains of earlier occupants dating from around 2000BC. If you have not had any exercise yet today, now is the time to pay your respects to Queen Maeve. The walk, following the signposted track, takes about 35 minutes. Even if you are not moved by the romance of the legend, it is worth the walk just to see the panoramas that sweep across Sligo Bay to the Ox Mountains in one direction and Benbulben in the other.

The Far West

6. WESTPORT *(see map p38)*

This trip divides into two parts: the morning is spent exploring Westport's 18th-century charms before heading north along the shore of Clew Bay to Croagh Patrick, Ireland's holiest mountain. A spectacular drive takes you to the village of Leenane, made famous by the movie *The Field*. After returning for lunch in one of Westport's superb fish restaurants, head west for the tropical ambience and wild flowers of Achill Island.

This is not one of those guidebooks that belittles **Westport's** classic looks. The tree-lined mall on either side of the Carrowbeg River and the spacious Octagon, the eight-sided market place with its radiating streets and its wide main boulevard, are its centrepieces. The town was specially designed at the end of the 18th century for the Marquess of Sligo. No-one quite knows who the architect was, but the elegant buildings, combining a sense of space and grace, hint towards an unknown Frenchman taken prisoner-of-war from General Humbert's ill-fated army of 1798. Another less fanciful view is that it was the well-known Georgian architect James Wyatt, who together with Richard Cassells also designed the jewel of the town, the 18th-century **Westport House** (hours vary, but always open 2–5pm Easter–Sept). The main house has a collection of landscape and portrait paintings but children prefer the grounds, zoo, leisurely boat-trips and picnics by the lake.

After you have explored Westport, your journey takes you west on the R335 along Clew Bay, which is peppered with inlets and islands. Some 10km (6¼ miles) out of Westport, on the left, is the car park for Ireland's holiest mountain, **Croagh Patrick**. This cone-shaped peak reaches almost 800m (2,600ft) towards the heavens and is where St Patrick is believed to have fasted during the 40 days of Lent in AD441. The cliff face above the car park is where St Patrick is said to have rung his bell to summon all of Ireland's venomous creatures, which he then cast into eternity via the precipice. The last Sunday in July, known as *Crom Dubh's* Sunday, is when pilgrims gather to make the arduous climb to the summit. Some people even climb barefoot in order to purge themselves of materialistic urges.

The road along Clew Bay, with its views of Clare Island, offers many

CAUTION

SHEEP CROSSING

Left: Carrowmore Dolmen. **Above:** at the base of Croagh Patrick
Right: sheep have right of way

turnings to small beaches divided by the rocks of the seashore. At **Louisburg** you can turn westward across the moorland road to **Roonah Quay**. This short scenic deviation offers the opportunity of a boat ride to mountainous **Clare Island**, with its harbour overlooked by the castle. This was once the fortress of the pirate queen Grace O'Malley, who preyed on cargo ships. Legends of her freebooting exploits, challenges to England's navy and subsequent allegiance to Queen Elizabeth I are still plentiful. Her grave is in the abbey on the island. Returning to Louisburg, turn right on the R335 and pass Doo Lough, a long silvery lake where mountains rise on both sides to over 700m (2,300ft). In the narrow defile, your breath may be taken away, not just by the beautiful landscape but also by the narrow passage which the road takes alongside the river. Descend to **Killary Harbour**, an inlet cut like a fjord into the surrounding mountains with **Leenane** at its head. Leenane, dominated by the Devil's Mother (650m/2,130ft) and hemmed in by sweeping slopes, has been made famous by the film, *The Field*, with Richard Harris. Hitherto it was one of Connacht's most secret waterside villages.

The N59 turns you back towards Westport, 32km (20 miles) away. Imposing as the journey is, between the Partry Mountains on the right and the Sheffry Hills opposite, the moorland road offers little incentive to punctuate the drive, so you should head straight for Westport anticipating a seafood lunch

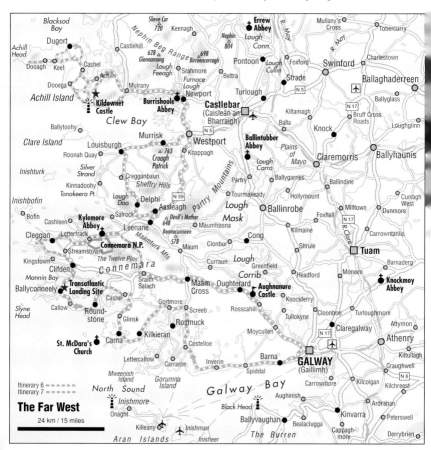

The Far West
Itinerary 6
Itinerary 7
24 km / 15 miles

at one of the restaurants on the quay overlooking Clew Bay. After lunch, leave Westport for **Newport** on the winding N59. This fine village rises above the river and is a fishing centre for the nearby loughs of Feeagh, Furnace and Beltra. Our first stop is at **Burrishoole Abbey** set on a small promontory where two creeks meet. It was founded in the 15th century by the Dominicans and is a charming, lonely ruin in a delightful setting.

Head on to Mulrany (also called Mallaranny) on the narrow isthmus that joins up with the Curraun Peninsula. The meeting of the two bays, coupled with the protection of the mountains, has created an extremely mild climate, particularly noticeable in spring, which brings an early show of wild flowers, and in late summer when the fuchsia bursts into bloom, boxing in homes with walls of shiny crimson pendulums. Giant sub-tropical gunnera plants have also lost their inhibitions here and rampage along ditches to vie with the bog itself. Once over the causeway bridge you arrive on **Achill Island** where you follow the Atlantic Drive signs taking you clockwise round the island. You'll pass several small sad cemeteries – a result of the 'great hunger' of the 1840s and shipping tragedies in Clew Bay. One is just before **Kildownet Castle** – a fine tower standing on the rocky beach. A little way on, the road takes to the cliffs and becomes a switchback, offering superb coastal views. To the south there are good views of Clare Island.

At Dooega (Dumha Eige) the road turns inland for 5km (3 miles) or so before turning left for Keel and Dooagh. **Keel** shows signs that, lonely as you might have imagined the road to be, other holidaymakers have come this way as well. The beach, with its giant caravan site, destroys the illusion of solitude. Further on is **Dooagh** with the famous Keem Strand backed by the peak of Croaghaun. This is also where Captain Boycott had a lodge. His name is now in the dictionary, because he was totally ostracised by local people when working as a landlord's agent in the 1770s. Charles Stewart Parnell coined his name to describe this tactic in the struggle against landlordism. Here the road ends and you can continue on a healthy walk to **Achill Head**, looking to the right to the 650-m (2,100-ft) cliff that rises out of the sea almost to the top of Croaghaun. Your journey back follows the Atlantic Drive route signs. To sample the tranquillity of the area, simply turn

Above: Leenane
Right: stacking turf

off and follow a side road, such as the one for **Dugort**. The way back also means sharing the road with sheep and cattle munching on the verges. There are areas where turf cutters can be seen gashing the peat. The journey offers views across Achill Sound and deep into County Mayo. The <u>road back</u> into Achill is thick with rhododendrons before we meet the causeway bridge, which takes us back via Mulrany to Westport.

7. CONNEMARA *(see map p38)*

This circular drive from Galway can be done in a day. If you adopt the more leisurely pace of rural Ireland, you could take two. It takes you through some of the strangest and most beautiful scenery in the far west of Ireland, a region with an unsurpassed sense of remoteness. Highlights include the Connemara National Park, the Alcock and Brown memorial and numerous timeless fishing villages.

'There is nowhere like Connemara', so the saying goes. To some the landscape is melancholic; to others it is distinctive, those for whom lonely scenery is the epitome of peace. **Connemara** offers itself openly to all interpretations. To one person's eye, the hallmarks are its shapes and colours; the varying pewter shades of ever-present water and stone; walls and rocky outcrops swelling out in lumps and bumps from an intense green turf, occasionally splashed white by a solitary cottage. To others it may be the variety of russets on the slopes of the rugged peaks of the Maamturk Mountains cut by so many valleys, lakes and rivers; or the flat, saw-toothed coastline of rocky promontories joined by sandy, shell-filled coves.

Aughnanure Castle

'Westward ho, let us rise with the sun and be off to the land of the west'. The first drive in Connemara takes you away from the buzz and bustle of Galway to Oughterard along the shores of mighty **Lough Corrib**. Drive along the N59 before turning right to visit **Aughnanure Castle** (late spring to end autumn, daily 9.30am–6.30pm), situated 25km (15½ miles) from the

city centre. This splendid castle, expertly restored, rests nobly beside a stream.

Return to the main road, turning right in Oughterard, then almost immediately left over the bridge, to begin a journey along the lakeshore with its inlets, islets and boathouses, set among wild fuchsia hedges.

The road ends after 12km (7½ miles) at a little-used car park beside the water. From here you can enjoy the splendid view of the Hill O'Doon as depicted on postcards.

Left: Aughnanure Castle

f a r   w e s t

Turning round, retrace your journey for 8km (5 miles), looking for a lane signposted 'Scenic Route' on your right. This cuts out the return to Oughterard and takes you cross-country, offering superb views. At the N59, turn right for **Maam Cross**. This remote hamlet set in the shadow of Leckavrea Mountain has a replica of the cottage used in the famous 1952 film, *The Quiet Man*. The town is the district centre for roadside markets and gatherings. Stop if something is going on as this is a wonderful chance to encounter local people, before continuing along the valley to **Sraith Salach** (also known as **Recess**). This hamlet, surrounded by lakes, has an excellent craft shop offering items made from local marble.

Kylemore Abbey
Next, turn right on the R344. The road gently climbs into the hills, over a saddle and down along the shores of Lough Inagh, a particularly beautiful drive. At the junction with the N59 turn left towards Letterfrack, following another valley with the **Twelve Pins** mountains on your left. The last of the three lakes that stretch 8km (5 miles) on the Dawros River reveals **Kylemore Abbey** (daily, 9am–5.30pm), which appears to grow from among the lakeshore trees in the mountain's shadow. Its many towers and battlements, built in the 1860s, reflect the grandeur and fantasy of brash Balmoral-Gothic architecture. Today it is a convent school run by Benedictine Nuns, but visitors can enjoy the renovated neo-Gothic church, as well as the restaurant and the shop selling the nuns' pottery and food products. About 1½km (1 mile) from the abbey there is a visitor centre and 2.5ha (6 acres) of Victorian gardens that are in the process of being restored.

Some 5km (3 miles) beyond lies **Letterfrack**, a delightful village at the head of Barnaderg Bay, founded by the Quakers in the 19th century. On your left is **Connemara National Park**, with its expanse of fine boglands, mountains and heaths. The visitor centre (Apr–Oct, daily) has a natural history audio-visual presentation and gives comprehensive details of the park's features from flora and fauna to geology, hiking trails and climbs. Your route now takes you out to Connemara, where rocky outcrops break out

Above: Maam Cross on market day

from the vivid greens of the turf and whitewashed cottages are tucked away among the boulders. This place fills one with a sense of remoteness and of wonder that anyone could till such tough and barren terrain. The true horror of Cromwell's ultimatum to the Irish, 'To Hell or to Connacht', becomes clear.

Fishing Villages

Some 3km (1¼ miles) out of Letterfrack, turn right following the sign to **Cleggan**, a fishing village where you can take a boat ride out to Inishbofin Island. Continue along the road around the peninsula, with its tiny sandy bays between rocky, seaweed-clad fingers that stretch far into the sea. Here, rock-pools are filled with shrimps, the wet sands are loaded with razor clams, while a probe beneath a seaweed-encrusted stone shelf might just reveal the dark iridescent hue of a tasty lobster.

Our peninsula circuit brings you next to **Clifden**, dominated by its two church spires, perched in a high mountain valley setting above an inlet of Ardbear Bay. This is the main town of Connemara, attracting artists, mountaineers, sea anglers, salmon fishermen, the famous Connemara pony breeders and marble stone masons. There is little of historic interest here, but it is worth staying a while just for the excellent restaurants serving local lobsters, oysters, langoustines and mussels. Whether or not you spend the night here, your journey now takes you south from Clifden on the R341.

Just beyond Ballyconneely is the **Alcock and Brown Transatlantic Landing Site**. This is a memorial commemorating the first transatlantic flight, made in the wood and fabric-covered Vickers Vimy. On 15 June 1919, the two aviators landed here, tipping their biplane onto its nose in the bog after 16 hours and 12 minutes of flight.

Continue along to **Roundstone** with Mount Errisbeg towering over its harbour. Like all of Connemara's fishing villages, there is little to see here in the way of ruins, little evi-

The Aran Islands

The Aran Islands, Inishmore (*Inis Mór*), Inishman (*Inis Meain*) and Inisheer (*Inis Oirr*) lying in the mouth of Galway Bay, were inhabited long before recorded history and contain many pre-Christian and early Christian remains. The most noteworthy, Dun Aengus (*Dún Aoinghusa*) on Inis Mór, is a 2,000-year-old Celtic dry-stone fort. Its semi-circular wall is perched on top of a 90-m (300-ft) sheer cliff, with breathtaking views. Irish Gaelic is the first language of the friendly islanders, but most speak fluent English as well.

You can travel to the islands by sea or air. **Island ferries**. (tel: 091-568903) operates daily sailings from Rossaveal to all three islands year round. Inis Oirr, the furthest island, can be reached in an hour. There are special rates for children and families. Flights to the islands take 10 minutes. **Aer Árran** (tel: 091 593034) operates daily flights year round from Connemara Regional Airport in Inverin. Special offers are available, which include one night's B&B on the island. Alternatively, you can fly one way and sail the other.

Above: fresh lobster
Right: Galway City

far west

dence of momentous history. These tiny places have had hardships enough without those of blood and battle. Even so, these villages are a picturesque joy to see and time can be spent dwelling upon their peaceful lifestyles. Beyond Roundstone lies Toombeola with its ruined abbey. Turn right onto the R342 to **Cashel**. The strange Connemara coastline still flanks the road. Peeling off onto any side track to the right will bring you to shell-encrusted beaches that are all your own, with not another soul in sight.

From the lobster port of Carna, the road sweeps around to **Kilkieran (Cill Ciaráin)** where St Kieran is said to have come ashore. His holy well in the cemetery is visited by pilgrims every September. Beyond lie Derryrush and Gortmore *(An Gort Mór)*. Within 3km (1¾ miles), turn right onto the R336 towards Costelloe *(Casla)*, which has a radio station that broadcasts only in Irish Gaelic. Continue along the north shore of Galway Bay, passing the turn-off to the right that leads to Rossaveal, the departure point for boats to the Aran Islands, and through the coastal village of Inverin *(Indreabhán)*, broadcasting home of TG4, the Gaelic TV station, and the base of Connemara Regional Airport, which has daily flights to the Arans (*see box, page 42*). Continue through Spiddal *(An Spidéal)* and Barna *(Bearna)*, before entering Galway again.

Galway City

Today **Galway** is a vigorous industrial and commercial centre. Its history is not yet lost and the focal point is the wide Eyre Square with its cascading fountain and the John F. Kennedy Park. The tourist office in the square has details of a number of walking tours that include the **Church of St Nicholas** (built 1320). It is said that Christopher Columbus prayed here before his epic voyage. Lynch's memorial window features a skull and crossbones and a plaque in memory of the merciless judge who condemned and hanged his own son in 1493 for the jealous murder of a visiting Spaniard. Lynch's Castle sadly underwent a horrific modernisation in the 1960s. Probably the most surprising sight in the city, whose yesterdays are fast being obscured, are the salmon waiting below **Salmon Weir Bridge** near the cathedral, before leaping the weir to make their way up to Lough Corrib to spawn.

8. THE BURREN *(see map below)*

This day-long itinerary takes you from Galway to Limerick across the glaciated uplands of The Burren, where there are 400 historic forts, and both arctic and tropical plants. Visit the Burren Display Centre, Kilfenora Cathedral and the high crosses, the spa town of Lisdoonvarna with its Festival of Match-Making, the Cliffs of Moher and Ennis Abbey before reaching Limerick, the major city in the mid-west of Ireland.

Leaving Galway southward by the N6 to Dublin then exiting onto the combined N18/N67 to Oranmore. You'll then pass the late Paddy Burke's tavern in **Clarinbridge** where he founded the world-famous Galway Oyster Festival, held each September. At Kilcolgan, branch right on the N67 for the curiosity of **Dunguaire Castle** (May–mid-Oct 9.30am–5.30pm). The 16th-century tower, in its idyllic waterside setting, specialises in hosting medieval banquets at which the guests are entertained by 'light-hearted' extracts from Synge, Yeats and Gogarty. The phrase 'light-hearted', in relation to these authors, seems a contradiction. Tel: 061-3615020 to book. The harbour is a delight and worthy of a pause for its traditional sailboats – Galway Bay hookers are often moored along the quay.

Aillwee Caves

Some 20km (12½ miles) on, we pass through Ballyvaughan, a lively seaside village, and head south on the R480 Corofin road to reach the **Aillwee Caves** (open daily year-round, limited tours Nov–Mar). It is said that the caves were discovered in 1896, although the story here is that a farmer found them by accident in 1944 while looking for his dog. Almost as impressive as the guided tour – through passages, into stalactitic chambers and past waterfalls – is the visitor centre itself. Moulded into the terrain, the stone-faced structure has won

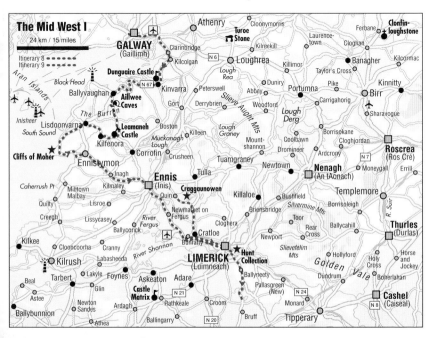

many awards. Before leaving the car park, look over the parapet down onto a string of earthen ring forts.

The Burren

Shortly beyond Aillwee, as you continue on the R480, you will enter the strangeness of **The Burren** with its swirling limestone terraces. This treeless plateau is an area, 500sq. km (200sq. miles) in size, of sedimentary limestone and shell from an ancient seabed that has risen 300m (1,000ft) and then suffered the tortures of glacial action. Smoothed by ice and the elements, the gnarled and fissured pavements have become home to a unique flora and fauna, while underground rivers rush below the surface, creating over 60km (37 miles) of known pot-holing tunnels and caverns. This was also a busy habitat for Neolithic man. Cairns, court graves and dolmens abound, including some 400 stone forts *(cashels)*. The only wonder is how they tilled such rock.

Over 125 different types of plant thrive here including 22 species of orchid. The Burren also has some unique butterfly species. Botanists from all over the world scurry around The Burren in springtime, amazed that plants from the four zones – Arctic, Alpine, Temperate and Tropical – flourish here side by side. May and June are the real months of glory, when the gentians, mountain avens and bloody cranesbills bloom.

The views to the right across Galway Bay are another sensation. Look out for herds of wild goat and the elusive pine marten. Another noticeable feature are the 'holed walls' that allow the wind through, differing in style every few hundred metres depending on the maker's style. Built during the famine of the 1840s, some enclosures are miniscule. Hereditary laws stated that land had to be bequeathed to every child in equal measure, so plots had to be divided into smaller and smaller allotments. The road takes us past the famous portal tomb, **Poulnabrone Dolmen**, dating back to 4,000BC.

Tourists are being asked to adopt a voluntary Burren protection code and not to build fake dolmens, which causes extensive damage. Please take nothing but photographs and leave nothing but your footprints.

As the road descends from the high Burren plateau, you will see **Lemenagh Castle**, stronghold of the O'Briens. The castle was built in two phases: the tower in 1480 and the manor in 1640. In 1651 Conor O'Brien's body was brought back from battle to the castle. Maura

Above: Aillwee Cave
Right: Burren boulders

Rua MacMahon, his colourful and notorious wife, refused the servants permission to take her dead husband inside, saying, 'We want no dead men here.' Rarely visited by tourists, it is well worth a look, especially the stone stairway in the tower. Turn right at this crossroad and take the R476 for **Kilfenora**, once an ecclesiastical capital. The **Burren Centre** (Mar–May and Sep–Oct 10am–5pm; Jun–Aug 9.30am–6pm) is a must: scale models of the region explain the geology, scenery, flora and fauna effectively through the medium of a sound and light show. They also cover many of the region's historical sites, which you would not otherwise see without tramping over the hills for weeks. The audio-visual presentation with commentary by well-known naturalist Eamonn de Buitlear is first-rate, as are the tea rooms on-site.

Adjacent to the display centre, in this tiny village, is the **cathedral**, founded on the monastery site of St Fachtnan in the 12th-century. The walls display carved effigies of bishops from the 13th and 14th centuries. There are four high crosses; the most interesting, the Doorty Cross, shows three bishops with different croziers. The journey now takes you on to **Lisdoonvarna**, a spa town popular in the Victorian era for its iron, magnesium and sulphur baths. The **Spa-Wells Health Centre** serves heated sulphur water for drinking, whilst the Bath House offers sauna and pampering treatments, followed by an old-time dance session (lunchtimes June–Oct 10am–6pm). In September the town goes in for a month-long party with its **Match-Making festival**. This is a legacy from the days when hard-working rural farmers came to town after the harvest for a little 'yo-ho' and, hopefully, to find a wife. For lunch, try the restaurant in Sheedy's Country House Hotel (tel: 065-7074026) where the locally sourced international menu is reliable.

The Cliffs of Moher and Ennis

From here, take the coast road to the **Cliffs of Moher**, one of County Clare's most renowned features. The cliffs rise 200m (650ft) vertically from the Atlantic breakers and stretch for some 7km (4¼ miles). There's an excellent view of the Aran Islands, with the varying colours of their rock strata. Looking down upon fulmars, kittiwakes, puffins, razorbills and rare choughs is a dizzying experience. The visitor centre has a café and a bureau de change.

Finally, take the R478 to **Ennistymon**, with its colourful shopfronts, scenic waterfall and the lively Archway Tavern, and on to the N85 to **Ennis** with its striking Franciscan Abbey (founded in 1250). In the museum, off O'Connell Square, the *Riches of Clare* exhibition traces 6,000 years of local history (9.30am–5.30pm, closed weekends Jan–Feb and Sun Mar–May and Oct–Dec). From here, head straight along the N18 to Limerick or, if you are feeling extravagant, to the luxurious Dromoland Castle Hotel (Newmarket-on-Fergus, 10km (6¼ miles) south of Ennis off the N18).

Above: the Cliffs of Moher

9. LIMERICK INTERLUDE *(see map p44)*

Thanks to Shannon International Airport, Limerick and environs have no shortage of tourist attractions. After the lonely beauty of Ireland's far west, the sights of Limerick may strike you as somewhat contrived. Even so, each sight has its merits, so relax and spend a day enjoying such themed introductions to Ireland's heritage as the Craggaunowen Project at Quin, the Bunratty Folk Park and Castle, the well-restored King John's Castle in Limerick and the Lough Gur Stone-Age Project.

The **Craggaunowen Project** (Apr and Sep–Oct 10am–6pm, May–Aug 9am–6pm, last admission 5pm), 3km (2 miles) from Quin (20km/12½ miles north of Limerick on the R469), is a re-creation of life in Neolithic times, inspired by the late historian and archaeologist John Hunt. The most striking feature is the **Crannóg**, or lake-dwelling complex, with its wattle and daub houses. There is also a ring fort with souterrain. There may once have been 40,000 similar settlements throughout Ireland. Another tableau is a cooking site of the type often used on hunting trips as well as in settlements. Pits were dug into the marshy ground where water would seep, and baked stones were thrown in to heat the water.

One genuine artefact is the 2,000-year-old wooden trackway removed for preservation from Longford. Also on display is a replica of a 6th-century boat, the *Brendan*, built by Tim Severin, who sailed it across the Atlantic in support of his theory that St Brendan reached the shores of the New World in the 6th century. A right turn towards Quin along the R469 brings you to **Knappogue Castle**. Built in 1467 by the powerful McNamaras, who also built Bunratty, it holds medieval banquets (Apr–Oct, 9.30am–5.30pm).

Bunratty

A stop at **Bunratty** 10km (6¼ miles) west of Limerick on the N18 is a thought-provoking experience. The castle (9.30am–4pm), dating back to 1277, has seen turbulent times and much fighting outside its walls. It has been rebuilt several times, but the present structure dates back to 1450. Like Craggaunowen, it has been restored and furnished with items befitting the period. Consider booking a place at the evening medieval banquet (year-round, subject to demand) – the best in Ireland – hosted by celebrated singers and entertainers.

The **Folk Park** in the castle grounds (daily year-round), depicts Irish lifestyles through the ages. Cottages have been furnished accurately, and there is an authentic 19th-century village with craft workshops and general stores in which the serving staff wear period costume. It is not that long ago – in fact just 50 years or so – since ranges replaced open fires and houses in the far west got electricity. Outside Bunratty is **Durty Nellie's Pub**, touristy but well worth visiting, as is the Bunratty Woollen Mills (opposite the castle).

Above: children on Clare Island

In Limerick itself, it is essential to see **King John's Castle** (Limerick Castle; daily year-round), a medieval fortress with an imaginative exhibition tracing the history of Limerick. Some 17km (10½ miles) south of the city, well signed from the R512, is **Lough Gur** (May–Sept 10.30am–6pm), one of the most important archaeological sites in Ireland, with evidence of man's existence here from 3000BC to medieval times.

10. LIMERICK TO TRALEE *(see map p50)*

A day-long journey southwards from Limerick visiting Adare, which is considered to be Ireland's loveliest village; Castle Matrix, where possibly the first potatoes in Ireland were cultivated; Ardagh, famous for its Chalice; Foynes with its Flying Boat Museum; and Castleisland with the Crag Cave system.

Before leaving Limerick, call in at the **Hunt Museum** (Custom House, Rutland Street; Mon–Sat 10am–5pm; Sun 2–5pm), which contains a fine collection of early Celtic treasures. Afterwards, spend some time walking the wide streets of the third-largest city in Ireland, founded by the Danes in the 9th century. Historically, it has had its sieges and battles from the time Brian Ború took it from the Danes. After the Battle of the Boyne in 1690, the Irish holed up in King John's Castle for over a year until surrendering with honour, after which the famous Treaty of Limerick was signed, beginning the exodus and banishment of Irish chiefs, nobles and soldiers, who became known as the 'Wild Geese'. Climb the tower for a view of the city.

There are excellent walking tours of Limerick, some of them guided; ask for details from the tourist office in Arthur's Quay (tel: 061-317522). From Limerick, travel southwest on the N20/N21 to **Adare (Ath Dara)**, an old-world village with an English look. Adare has three abbeys: the Trinitarian Abbey, founded in 1230, is partly restored and in use; the Augustinian Priory dates to 1315; and the Franciscan Friary (built 1464) now stands at the heart of the Golf Club, along with Desmond Castle.

Cruising

Ireland has the largest expanse of waterways in Europe dedicated solely to boating and fishing. A chain of lakes and rivers stretches from Beleek in County Fermanagh to Killaloe in County Clare – a distance of 483km (300 miles). You are free to travel at your own pace along these quiet, traffic-free waterways; to stop and explore the countryside or to anchor in the middle of a lake and fish for days. Time loses all meaning as you drift in total silence along meandering rivers into the vastness of great lakes such as Upper Lough Erne between Beleek and Belturbet, or Lough Ree or Lough Derg on the Shannon.

You can drop anchor anywhere and go for a meal ashore, or join in a traditional music night at one of the pubs in the many friendly villages lying along the banks of the river. **Waveline Cruises** (tel: 09064-85711) and **Emerald Star** (tel: 07196 27693) operate along the Shannon Erne waterway.

If you'd rather be a passenger than a skipper, there are several companies that operate cruises on the River Shannon (**Moon River Pleasure Cruiser**, tel: 07196-21777) and on Lough Key in County Westmeath (**Bernie and Pete Walsh**, tel/fax: 07196-67037). On Lough Gill, the **Wild Rose Waterbus** (tel: 07191-64266) will take you to the Lake Isle of Inisfree. Barge tours of the Grand Canal are run by the **Galley Cruising Restaurant** (tel: 051-421723) will provide you with a good-quality meal as you cruise along the Barrow.

f a r w e s t

Smooth countryside lies alongside the N21 to **Rathkeale** where there are the remains of an Augustinian priory. **Castle Matrix**, 3km (1¾ miles) along on the right, is privately owned by Sean O'Driscoll, an American architect who has restored the castle and furnished it authentically*. Back on the N21, turn right for **Ardagh** where, in 1868, the famous Celtic chalice and brooch (now in Dublin's National Museum) were discovered in the nearby ring fort, accessible by crossing a field. In contrast is **Foynes**, our next stop. Here is the **Foynes Flying Boat Museum** (daily, Apr–Oct 10am–6pm), which takes its theme from the age of the transatlantic flying boats and the great Pan American clippers of the 1930s.

Glin Castle

Continue alongside the Shannon Estuary to **Glin** with its magical castle (rooms available from Mar–Nov; tel: 068-34173), built in 1780s, though the embellishments, such as the battlements and mullioned windows, were added in the 1820s. It is owned by the Fitzgeralds, hereditary Knights of Glin.

Further along the shore is **Tarbert**, where ferries leave for County Clare. **Tarbert House** is true Georgian-Irish. There is an excellent collection of period furniture, including Irish Chippendale, and portraits by Irish artists. At the restored **Tarbert Bridewell courthouse and jail**, you can learn how justice was administered in 19th-century Ireland (daily Apr–Oct 10am–6pm).

Next, turn inland on the N69 to **Listowel**, a market town with the remains of a twin-towered Fitzmaurice castle in the square. The town is proud of having produced many nationally acclaimed writers, and stages a well-known literary festival every June.

Continue by taking the R555 to **Abbeyfeale**, then turn right on the N21 to **Castleisland**, a bustling town, which was once the stronghold of the Desmonds. Turn right by the library and the road leads to the **Crag Cave** (daily Mar–Nov) where some 4km (2½ miles) of limestone caves have been surveyed. There is a visitor centre and the guided tour weaves amongst the stalactites and stalagmites. When you've seen enough, return to Castleisland and take the N21 to Tralee.

Above: King John's Castle, Limerick
Right: statue of the Virgin Mary, Kilmalkedar

11. THE DINGLE PENINSULA *(see map below)*

This is one of Ireland's most spectacular tours. The road from Tralee takes you onto the stunning Dingle Peninsula, where Irish Gaelic is the first language and 2,000 sites of antiquity have been identified. Notable

are the stone beehive huts built by the early monks and the Gallarus Oratory. The return journey crosses the Connor Pass where there are dramatic vistas. If based in Killarney, Cork or Tralee, you may opt for an organised tour which covers the same route, with the exception of the Connor Pass. If doing this route by car, expect misleading signposting, with incorrect distances marked and many names written only in Irish.

At the Ashe Memorial Hall in Denny Street, the *Kerry the Kingdom* exhibition traces the history of Kerry specifically, and Ireland generally, from the earliest times. After exploring Denny Street and the 18th-century architecture of the centre of **Tralee**, head west on the N86. The first point of interest is the **Blennerville Windmill and Visitor Centre** (Apr–Oct 10am–6pm), beside the old ship canal. This living reminder of Ireland's industrial past is featured in the *Guinness Book of Records* as the largest working windmill in these islands. An exhibition also highlights the village's role as an embarkation point for immigrants heading to North America during the famine. Beyond, the journey's beginning seems unpromising as you run along the

bland marshy edges of Tralee Bay for some 15km (9¼ miles). However, at **Camp**, the left turn sees you start to climb, offering a view sweeping from Castlegregory to Rough Point and onto Tralee Bay. Ascending the side of the mountain of Caherconree, you see an ancient fort on the summit – the home of legendary hero-god, Curio Mac Daire.

Take the next left to see **Inch**, the beach featured in the film *Ryan's Daughter*, with its ancient sandhill dwellings. Today it is better known as the location of the infamous liaison between

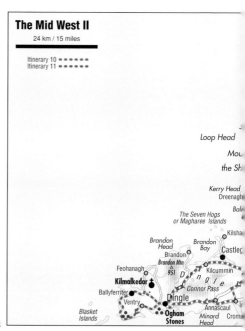

The Mid West II

24 km / 15 miles

Itinerary 10 ●●●●●●
Itinerary 11 ●●●●●●

Loop Head

Mou

the Sh

Kerry Head
Dreenagh

The Seven Hogs
or Magharee Islands

Bal

Kilsha

Brandon
Head   *Brandon*
            Bay   *Castle*

Brandon
Brandon Mtn
951   *D n g l e*   *Kilcummin*

Feohanagh

Kilmalkedor ✝

Ballyferriter ●   *Connor Pass*

Ventry   **Dingle**

Blasket
Islands   **Oghám**   *Annascaul*
              Stones   *Minard* *Croma*
                           Head

Above: sheep on the Dingle Peninsula

f a r   w e s t

Bishop Casey and an American woman. The discovery of their love child in 1992 had long-lasting social reverberations. Proceed to **Annascaul** where the South Pole Inn (tel: 066-9157388) recalls that a former proprietor was a member of the ill-fated Scott expedition to the Antarctic. Carry on towards Dingle (An Daingean). At **Ballintaggart**, turn left and sharp left again at a 'Road Danger' sign to see a small round Celtic cemetery with nine Ogham stones.

Dingle Town

Back to the route, drive into **Dingle** town, which enjoys new-found wealth as a result of all the visitors who come to see Fungie, the dolphin that came to the harbour in 1985 and has been there ever since. Local boatmen offer dolphin-spotting trips from Dingle pier (tel: 066-9152626). You can visit the **Dingle Oceanworld Aquarium Mara Beo** (daily 10am–6pm; tel: 066-9152111; last admission an hour before closing), which has over 100 different species of fish and a walk-through tunnel tank. There's not much else to see, which may be why Marie Antoinette refused to be rescued from her French jail and brought here, where she was to be secretly housed in the property on the corner of John and Main streets. You may want to stop for shopping or lunch, if only to sample the arty-crafty atmosphere. Try **Doyle's Seafood Bar** (John Street; tel: 066-9151174) for excellent and inexpensive dishes.

From Dingle head out towards **Slea Head** on the R539, past Ventry Harbour with its complicated legends of kings, eloping wives, giants, champions, secret trysts, treachery and poets that put the legends of King Arthur to shame by comparison. At **Dunbeg**, some 6km (3¾ miles) from Ventry, is one of the region's many Iron-Age coastal forts with a souterrain and stone enclosures. At **Fahan** and for the next 5km (3 miles), over 400 *clochans* or beehive cells are scattered some 100m (300ft) above on the right-hand side of the road. They are accessible via farmers' gates – for a small fee, of course.

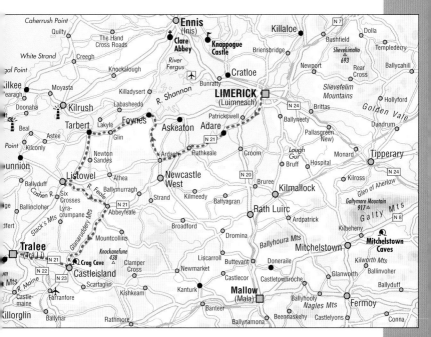

The Blasket Islands and Connor Pass

Follow the narrow coast road around **Slea Head**, gazing at coves, beaches and the **Blasket Islands**. The islanders are great storytellers and have made a lasting contribution to Irish literature. The Dunquin (Dún Chaoin) Ferry (066-9156422) makes regular half-hourly trips to the now uninhabited Great Blasket island (**An Bhlascaoid Mhóir**) in the summer (weather permitting). There is a hostel, café and craft shop on the island and tourists regularly camp here in summer. The **Great Blasket Centre** (tel: 066-9156444; Easter–Oct 10am–6pm, Jul–Aug until 7pm) is a labyrinth full of old archives and photographs.

After **Ballyferriter** (**Baile an Fheirtéaraigh**), follow the road inland. Some 3km (1¾ miles) beyond the village is the monastic settlement of **Reask**, which can be found by turning right after the bridge. Look out for its exquisitely cut Pillar Stone. From here, go back to the road and turn right, following the **Gallarus Oratory** signs. Dating from the 8th century, this endearing, upturned boat-shaped structure of unhewn stone was once a chapel. From here, look for a view of **Gallarus Castle**, a 15th-century tower house near the shore.

At the crossroads above Gallarus turn left for the ruined Romanesque **Kilmalkedar Church**. It was built around 1150, although the settlement dates from the 7th century. A number of curious standing stones exist, including an *Abecedarium* (a Latin alphabet stone), a holed stone, a sundial stone and

a crude ancient cross. The superbly carved Romanesque features have hardly weathered at all over the centuries.

Turning back past Gallarus, return to Dingle and turn left in the town for the precarious **Connor Pass**, the highest in Ireland. Even if it is misty you should still make this drive as the weather can be very different on the other side of the peninsula. At the summit you will be rewarded by one of Europe's most spectacular views; or, as one awed American visitor put it, a panorama 'in the world league…'

Above: Dingle Peninsula. **Right:** vintage transport
Left: Kilmalkedar Church and sundial stone

The Southwest

12. KILLARNEY TO BANTRY *(see map below)*

A full day that begins in Killarney, takes you to Muckross House for a horse-drawn car jaunt, then to Ross Castle, Glengarriff and the island paradise of Ilnacullin Gardens and finally to Bantry. If you are tired of driving, take a Lakes of Killarney minibus from Dero's in Main Street, Killarney (tel: 064-31251).

'Top of the morning to you!' If this phrase was ever used in Ireland then Killarney would be the most likely place to expect such a greeting. To get some perspective on this most friendly region, drive to the north end of the town by following the signs to **Aghadoe** for some 3km (2 miles). From here, panoramic views stretch some 20km (12½ miles) across island-studded **Lough Leane** and on to **Macgillycuddy's Reeks**.

Killarney town has a neo-Gothic **cathedral** and bustling narrow streets, with shops open until 10pm in summer. Consider lunch or dinner at Bricín, a homely traditional restaurant in the High Street – or drinks and traditional music in Buckley's Bar in College Street. South of the town, on the N71, is the beginning of **Killarney National Park** and the Muckross Estates. Turn right along the Ross Road to see **Ross Castle** (tel: 064-35851/2; Apr–Sept

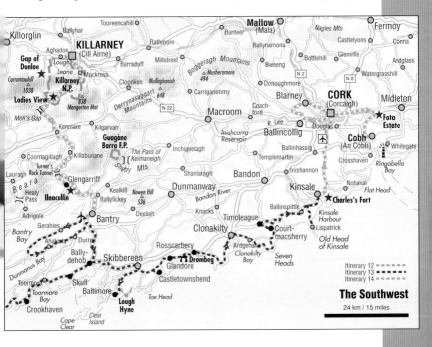

daily; Oct closed Mon; last admission 45 minutes before closing) on the shores of Lough Leane. Built in the 15th century, it was the stronghold of the O'Donoghue Ross chieftains for more than a century. In the 17th century, it was one of the last castles to fall to Cromwell.

Muckross Estate

Returning to the N71, take another right turn for **Muckross Abbey**, founded by a Franciscan order in 1448, where some of Ireland's greatest poets are buried. **Muckross House** (1843), a short distance further on, has elegant reception rooms, a restaurant and a working Folk Museum (Mar–Oct) where visitors can see yesterday's ways of bookbinding, basket-weaving, harness-making, shoe-cobbling and farming.

A horse-drawn jaunting car ride is highly recommended. A spin in a carriage – starting either in Killarney or at Muckross – takes you to Muckross Abbey and House, and then around the lakes and up the old mountain ways to **Torc Waterfall**. In spring, with the shrubs in full flower and the arboretum bursting into blossom, this is the way to see Muckross.

Back in the car, proceed on to Kenmare along the N71, enjoying the magnificent scenic drive that begins with walls of rhododendron hedging at Muckross, skirts the shores of Muckross Lake, then passes into a wild glen where scrub birches grow among lichen-covered rocks. Next comes a high climb to **Lady's View** (named after Queen Victoria) for a look back up the Killarney Valley, then a stretch of rich bogland before the descent into **Kenmare**, a genteel estate town built in 1773.

Situated where the Roughty River meets the sea, this town thrived on iron smelting, then became famous for lace and needlepoint. Its history goes further back, as you can see at the **Kenmare Heritage Centre** (Easter–Sept), located in the square at the tourist office. Com-

Above: Muckross House. **Right:** the younger generation. **Facing page:** Bantry House

The Ring of Kerry

You can drive non-stop around the 112 miles (180 km) of the popular Ring of Kerry in about four hours, but allow a full day if you want to make stops. The circuit is justifiably famous for its combination of lush, sub-tropical vegetation and rugged seascapes. Killorglin, a busy village, hosts the traditional Puck Fair, now chiefly a drinking festival, on 10–12 August. The main market town is Cahersiveen, which has a slightly dilapidated charm and a visitor centre housed in an exotic white-turreted building rumoured to have been designed for India. In mid-summer the Ring's narrow road can be clogged by cars and coaches, and many prefer the 30-mile (48-km) **Ring of Beara** to the south; skirting the north side of Bantry Bay, it also has impressive scenery – but less traffic.

ing out of Kenmare, climb away from the Sheen Valley. Known as the 'Tunnel Road', the N71 route often clings to the mountainside where massive rock formations have been bored through, some needing headlights to negotiate. Then comes a sweeping descent with a vista over the creeks, islands and inlets of Glengarriff and the vastness of Bantry Bay and the Sheep's Head Peninsula. On a fine day in **Glengarriff**, on the motionless water in the islet-dotted creeks, boats look like statues frozen to their moorings.

Fans of formal gardens should make time for **Ilnacullin** (daily year-round, hours vary; boat fare is separate from admission fee to Ilnacullin), the 15-hectare (38-acre) garden on **Garinish Island**. This is reached by boat from the harbour and you may enjoy the antics of playful seals on the way. Ilnacullin is an exotic formal garden. The island, barren until the early 20th century,was landscaped by Harold Peto.

13. FROM BANTRY TO KINSALE *(see map p53)*

From Bantry this scenic journey to Kinsale takes the Goat's Path Trail across the Sheep's Head Peninsula before going to colourful Skibbereen and Baltimore. This is followed by a coastal drive to Kinsale via Timoleague Abbey. Kinsale makes a lovely base for exploring the area *(see also itinerary 14)*.

Bantry is a delightful port at the head of the bay of the same name. **Bantry House** (Mar–Oct, daily 9am–6pm), ancestral home of the White family, is a superb mansion overlooking the bay. The tiered Italianate gardens are lovely, and the restored sections of the house are both intimate and eccentric. Treasures include tiled floors pillaged from Pompeii and the Marie Antoinette tapestries. Most enjoyable are the Italian-style gardens, now being restored with boxed parterres, lawns and antique urns set above the bay. In the old stables the *1796 French Armada Exhibition* explores the ill-fated invasion of December 1796.

On leaving Bantry southward you will find the signs directing you round the scenic **Goat's Path Trail**. This drive follows the very edge of the **Sheep's Head Peninsula** with views across the bay to the backdrop of the Caha Mountains on the Beara Peninsula. In autumn the ankle-high dwarf furze gleams pure gold against the dying brown heather blooms.

The return journey on the peninsula's south side at sea level offers a totally different coastline of low rocky promontories with sheltered waters in the inlets. Just past the village of **Ahakista** is a memorial garden for those lost in the sabotaged Air India 747 that went down off this coast in 1985. At Durrus take the R581 towards Goleen. Take a right-hand detour here to visit Ireland's most southwesterly point, the **Mizen Head Signal Fog and Visitor's Centre** at Cloughane Island (mid-Mar–Sept daily; Nov–mid-Mar weekends). A suspension bridge connects the island to the mainland, offering stunning views. An equally spectacular beach awaits you on your drive back.

Skibbereen

Following our route back to Ballydehob, turn right again for **Skibbereen**, possibly the most colourful town in Ireland. The buildings are like a string of Celtic jewels that jar, then delight the eye with agreeable surprise, especially on a drab rainy day. The Heritage Centre has an exhibition on the Great Famine of the 1840s and also houses the Lough Hyne Visitor Centre, which explains the unique nature of this marine reserve with its many Mediterranean-type species.

You may first wish to stop for a filling home-cooked lunch at the West Cork Hotel, Ilen Street (tel: 028-21277), or to try the lobster or scallops at Chez Youen (tel: 028-20136) in **Baltimore**, 13km (8 miles) southwest of Skibbereen. Raided by Algerian pirates in 1631, Baltimore is a fishing and sailing centre with ferries to Cape Clear and Sherkin Island.

Instead of heading directly back to Skibbereen, take the cross-country road 6km (3¾ miles) to view **Lough Hyne**. From here proceed to **Castletownshend** on the R596, where Edith Somerville and Violet Martin – better known as Somerville and Ross, the co-authors of *Some Experiences of an Irish RM* (1899) – lived. They are buried in the Church of Ireland graveyard overlooking the coast.

Back on the N71, turn right towards Glandore (R597), a sailing centre. Beyond is **Drombeg**, a stone circle dated to about the time of Christ. To the west of the circle are the remains of round huts, one of which contains a cooking trough where water was heated with hot stones, and food, wrapped in straw, was boiled. Follow the R597 through Rosscarbery and take the N71 to Clonakilty. Here the R600 leads to to the ruins of the 14th-century Franciscan **Timoleague Abbey**. From here the road winds alongside the muddy estuary, with its plethora of wading birds, before turning inland to the fertile farmlands outside Kinsale. To round off the day, why not go out and back onto another peninsula. **The Old Head Of Kinsale** is attractive at any time, but especially at sunset. On 7 May 1915, some 25km (15½ miles) offshore, the transatlantic liner *Lusitania* was torpedoed, introducing the United States into the Great War of 1914–18. It is said that local people witnessed the event from the Old Head. Accesss has to be arranged via the Old Head Golf Club (tel: 021 477 8444).

Above: Mizen Head

14. KINSALE AND COUNTY CORK *(see map p53)*

A day's itinerary circling Cork, starting in Kinsale, (the 'gourmet capital' of Ireland), including kissing the Blarney Stone plus touring the arboretum at Fota and the port of Cobh.

Kinsale is a picturesque town with its harbour and yachting marina, narrow streets and almshouses. Much has happened here that has influenced the history of Ireland: Kinsale saw the defeat of the Irish chiefs in 1601, and it was from here, after the Treaty of Limerick, that the banishment of the 'Wild Geese' began. This event meant the exile of all the Irish chiefs, many of whom went to fight for the armies of France and Spain. A few became known as 'wine geese' because they took to grape-growing in Cognac, Bordeaux and Burgundy. Today their names are known across the world: Hennessey, Delamain, Galway, Laughton, Barton, Dillon…

Castles and Forts

The story of these pioneers is documented in **Desmond Castle** on Cork Street (Easter–Jun Tues–Sun 10am–6pm, Jun–Oct daily 10am–6pm). It was from here that the buccaneer Alexander Selkirk sailed on the epic voyages that stranded him on a desert island – the inspiration for *Robinson Crusoe*.

This, and other aspects of the town's history, are covered by the **Kinsale Regional Museum and Courthouse** (Apr–Oct 10am–6pm daily, tel: 021-4777930). Formerly the Market House, it was built in the Dutch style in 1599 and has Ireland's largest collection of marine artefacts.

After a coffee stop at Kieran's Folkhouse Inn, in nearby Guardwell, stroll around the corner to St Multose Church with its Romanesque doorway and tower with the town stocks on display in the porch. **Charles Fort** (Mar–Oct, daily 10am–6pm;

Above: Kinsale Harbour
Right: Blarney Castle, County Cork

Nov–mid-Mar, weekends 10am–5pm) is the massive star-shaped fortress constructed in 1680 to the southeast of the town – the largest and best-preserved in Ireland. It overlooks Kinsale Harbour and the ruins of **James Fort**, an earlier construction, marooned on a tongue of land. After Charles Fort, enjoy a well-deserved lunch in Kinsale, a leisurely and memorable gourmet experience.

Blarney

Cork is not very far away, but little is left of the medieval city. Even the cathedral of St Finbar is Victorian-Gothic. Let us proceed instead around the city to **Blarney Castle** (9am–sundown, Mon–Sat, Sun from 9.30am May–Oct) and kiss the stone for the 'eloquence that will come into our tongues', by lying down, tilting the head backward over the castle wall whilst being held securely by David, Christy or Nigel. They handle some 300,000 kissers a year. The 15th-century castle is essentially a traditional tower house surrounded by an atmospheric 'Druidic' dell and rock garden. The village and its green, despite all the hordes of tourists, still has immense appeal. Shopping here is a serious activity, as this is the home of the **Blarney Woollen Mills** and the town has the greatest concentration of craft shops in the whole of Ireland.

For something more soothing drive back towards Cork, then east on the N25 for some 10km (6¼ miles) until the right turn for **Fota Estate**, **Arboretum** (year round) and **Wildlife Park** (summer daily; winter weekends). The former was developed over 200 years ago by the Smith-Barry family. There are over 1,000 species of shrubs and trees set in 32 hectares (82 acres), each labelled with botanical and English names with their dates of planting.

Turning right out of Fota we cross a delightful stone bridge where there is a castle tower on the left. For the next 6km (3¾ miles) the roadside scenery, sad to say, is an ecological disaster, consisting mainly of petrochemical plants. But persevere until you arrive in **Cobh** (pronounced 'cove').

If you are here on a Sunday (May–Sept) around 4.30pm you will be treated to an hour-long recital of the 49-bell carillon atop the spiky spired St Colman's Cathedral. If not, you won't miss them entirely because they ring out three times a day every day, but only for a few minutes.

Cobh is home base for the world's oldest yacht club, founded in 1720, the Royal Cork. In its great days, it saw all the famous Atlantic liners with the grandeur of their upper-deck life and the terrible tears of the famine-ravished, steerage emigrants. The major attraction in Cobh is the **Queenstown Story** (daily 10am–6pm, Nov–Mar closing at 5pm, last admission an hour before closing), which is located within Cobh station. This multimedia exhibition tells the story of a seafaring past and the suffering caused by Irish emigration. Since Cobh was the last port of call for the *Titanic*, a number of exhibits refer to the tragedy of the 'unsinkable' liner. The churchyard holds many of the nearly 2,000 victims of the *Lusitania*, sunk in dubious circumstances by a German submarine during World War I, and a statue on the seafront commemorates the tragedy.

Left: telling the Queenstown story
Right: a walk in the countryside

The Southeast

15. CORK TO WATERFORD *(see map below)*

A countryside, and latterly a coastal, drive from Cork to Waterford taking in Mallow; the woods and vales in the Blackwater Valley; the gardens of Anne's Grove; the Labbacallee Megalithic passage tomb; Glanworth; Fermoy and Lismore, with its lordly castle beneath the Knockmealdown Mountains; then on to Youghal; Dungarvan and finally to Waterford.

From Cork, head north to Mallow, where you may choose to stop at **Mallow Castle** to see the herd of white deer, some of which may well be descendants of the bucks given by England's first Queen Elizabeth. Your main objective, however, lies beside the N72 eastwards towards Fermoy and you must turn right just before the main street in Mallow. Some 12km (7½ miles) out of Mallow you will arrive at **Anne's Grove**, a Georgian country manor at Castletownroche. This well-proportioned house is the home of Mr and Mrs Annesley, descendants of the gardens' creator. There are a dozen gardens based on one of three themes – woodland, formal and river – where exotic plants are blended informally with native species.

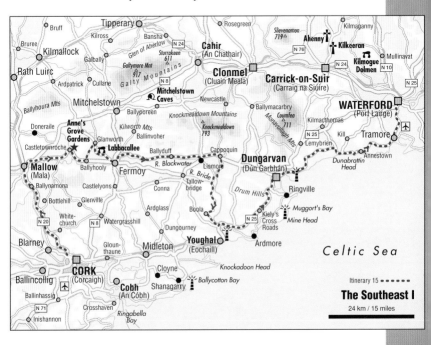

From Anne's Grove you could take country roads across to Glanworth but that would mean missing **Bridgetown Abbey**, a turning to the right some 3km (1¾ miles) from Castletownroche back on the N72. This Augustinian priory, in its tranquil river setting, is much in need of basic repair and notices warn of crumbling masonry. Returning to the N72 make a left turn, at a village with the roisterous-sounding name of **Bal-lyhooly**, to **Glanworth**. Here is Ireland's oldest stone bridge, built in 1600, with the ruins of the 13th-century Roche Castle towering up over the river. Coupled with a restored watermill and the ruins of a Dominican friary, it is a film set where the only missing elements are the actors. Some 3km (1¾ miles) to the south of the village is the **Lab-bacallee** wedge tomb. Finds here include early Bronze-Age material and pottery. On the way you pass the fine, but broken, tower of Teampall Lobhair.

Towards Lismore Castle

Fermoy, which you will soon reach but not enter, is a market town straddling the River Blackwater. The salmon ladder at the bridge always attracts a crowd of gazers after a good rainstorm to see the fish leaping their way upstream during spawning season. Turn left before the bridge, following the R666 along the Blackwater's north bank, through woods and meadows with pastures sloping gently away.

A few kilometres before you reach Lismore is a pull-in with a sign saying 'Towers'. Here is an opportunity to stretch your legs on a 20-minute round

trip across a field or two. The sight you have come to see consists of two flamboyant gatehouses sitting bizarrely in the middle of nowhere. The story goes that a lady, trying to outdo her wealthy in-laws, plagued her husband for the grandest house. He was bankrupted having built only the servants' lodges.

Lismore, dominated by the massive castle of the Duke of Devonshire, had, from the 7th century, one of the most renowned universities in Europe, founded by St Carthach (also known as St Cartach or even St Carthage). This scholarly city was sacked, pillaged and plundered 17 times over 600 years. It reached its height under St Colman in the 10th century with 20 sites of learning. Today more mystery remains than fact. The medieval-looking castle (grounds open Apr–Sept daily) has very little originality having been built in 1814, but it must rate as the most romantic-looking in all Ireland.

Continue to **Cappoquin**, a market town and centre for sport fishing, then turn right and southwards towards the town of **Youghal** (pronounced *yawl*) by the wooded and deep-cut Blackwater gorge. This historic seaport has an unusual clock tower that doubles as a gatehouse (built 1777). From the clock tower, stroll down North Man Street to see a cluster of historic buildings. On the left is the Red House, a gabled Dutch affair and, next door, battered Elizabethan almshouses. Just left in William Street, visit Myrtle Grove, a delightful Tudor manor reputedly once owned by Sir Walter Raleigh. It was here that John Huston's 1956 film *Moby Dick*, starring Gregory Peck as Captain Ahab, was made, and many stills from the movie are displayed in the quayside pub.

From Youghal, head east on the N25 to **Dungarvan**, with its 12th-century ruined castle, inside of which the restored barracks houses an exhibition. Ongoing restoration work may restrict access (Mon–Fri 10am–1pm and 2–5pm, open Sat May–Sep only). Just north of the town, at the junction for Cappoquin and Clonmel, is a monument to Master McGrath, a champion greyhound. Beaten only once in his career, he won the Waterloo Cup three times between 1868 and 1871.

Waterford *(see also itinerary 17)*

Finally, head onwards to **Tramore** on the R675, one of Ireland's most popular seaside resorts, with miles of sandy beaches, and on to **Waterford** city itself. Like neighbouring Wexford, Waterford was a Viking town and sections of the city walls remain from those times. The most intriguing of these is **Reginald's Tower** (daily, hours vary; tel 051-304500 for opening times). Built on a Viking site, this 12th-century Norman tower was the meeting place of Strongbow and his future wife, Aoife, daughter of the traitor Dermot McMurrough, King of Leinster – the marriage was arranged to consolidate the alliance between them.

Above left: the Labbacallee wedge tomb. **Below left:** Youghal clock tower
Above: eating on the hoof

16. CASHEL AND KILKENNY *(see map below)*

This circular day-long itinerary takes you from Waterford to the religious complex of the Rock of Cashel, once the seat of the Munster Kings, and to the prosperous medieval town of Kilkenny. It is a day spent exploring fabled ecclesiastical wonders, depicting the wealth and power of the pre-Reformation Church, and for enjoying some of Ireland's most stately castles.

From Waterford, take the N24 and drive 27km (16¾ miles) to **Carrick-on-Suir**, on a very pretty stretch of the Suir River. The 16th-century Ormond Castle (Jun–Sept 9.30am–6.30pm, access by guided tour) is said to be the birthplace of Ann Boleyn and is the best example in Ireland of an Elizabethan manor house. Some 10km (6¼ miles) to the north of the town are the high crosses at Ahenny, worth the drive if you are interested in Celtic sculpture.

Otherwise, continue towards Clonmel, the nation's centre for greyhound racing, perhaps stopping at the small factory shop of **Tipperary Crystal** (daily year-round) on the outskirts of Carrick on the N24. Tours of the factory are conducted so you can see the master glass blowers at their work. Continue then to **Cahir** (pronounced *care*), which has a magnificent castle surrounded by flour mills on the banks of the Suir (daily, hours vary; last admission 45 minutes before closing), which has an audio-visual presentation giving an overview of historical and archaeological monuments throughout the ages. This well-restored stronghold itself dates back to the 13th century. After admiring the three wards, clamber along the battlements for a good view.

The Rock of Cashel

Your next destination is the **Rock of Cashel** (daily, hours vary; last admission 45 minutes before closing; group tours should book in advance). This

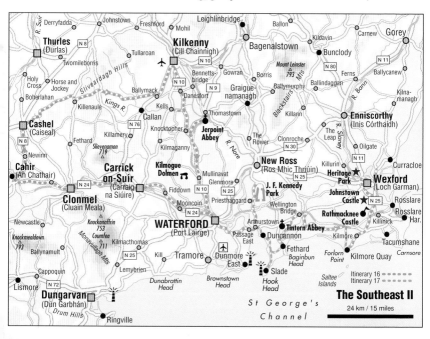

site's popularity may cause delays, especially in high season. Take the N8 from Cahir northbound for some 18km (11¼ miles) and it cannot be missed. The town hall is worth visiting for its museum and there are interesting craft shops. But it is the majesty of the cluster crowning the 63-m (206-ft) limestone outcrop, rising from the Tipperary Plain that has drawn you here today. This was probably once a centre of Druidic worship, but by the 4th-century AD it was the seat of the Kings of Munster. According to legend, it was here that St Patrick baptised King Aengus, and it was granted to the Church in 1101. Entrance is via the Hall of the Vicars Choral, the only isolated structure. The Round Tower is thought to date from the 12th century; the 14th-century cathedral is now roofless.

The real gem is **Cormac's Chapel**, built in the Romanesque style, considered one of Europe's finest chapels and begun in 1127. It is strangely sited alongside the cathedral, but askew of due east to meet the sunrise on St Cormac's day. The stone beneath the high cross is thought to be the one upon which the ancient kings were crowned. The entire complex was eventually abandoned in the middle of the 18th century. From the rock, if you are a view addict, let the eye wander across Tipperary's sweeping grasslands. To the southwest is the far-off grandeur of the Galtees; to the south lie the Knockmealdowns and to the southeast are the Comeraghs.

Kilkenny

From this literal high spot, drive straight to Kilkenny on the R691, joining the N76 for the final 11km (6¾ miles). Founded as a monastic settlement by St Canice in the 6th century, **Kilkenny** is a city that has thrived for well over 1,000 years. It remains extremely prosperous and little-changed. The place to start is the **Shee Alms House** (Rose Inn Street), built by a Tudor benefactor, which

is also the home of the tourist office (Apr–Sept, daily; Oct–Mar, Mon–Sat; official tours several times a day by Pat Tynan – pre-book for large groups. tel: 056-7751500).

Dominating the city are the grey stone turreted towers of **Kilkenny Castle** (daily, hours vary). Seat of the Butler family, the Dukes of Ormond, this stately castle is set in rich parklands. It was built in the 13th century, and has been altered over the years, but is now splendidly restored. The present building dates from 1820. A walk from the castle into the High Street

Above: the Rock of Cashel
Right: farming country

brings you to the arcaded 18th-century **Tholsel (Town Hall)**. Further on is **Rothe House** (daily, all year). Built in 1610 by John Rothe, a tudor merchant, it is now the headquarters of the archaeological society, with fine courtyards and a Costume Museum.

Still walking along the High Street, you can turn left into Blackmill Street for **Black Abbey**, an over-restored Dominican abbey, and on to **St Canice's Cathedral** (Mon–Sat 9am–6pm; Sun 2–6pm; closes 4pm Oct–Easter). The cathedral dates from 1285 and has fine medieval monuments, effigies, altar tombs and other sculptures. One of the most interesting exhibits is a scale model of the city as it was in the 17th century. The 6th-century round tower in the cathedral's grounds is the only remnant of St Canice's monastery.

If you enjoy shopping for Irish goods – such as linen, pewter, whiskey, knitwear, glass and crystal – then visit the celebrated **Kilkenny Design Centre**, which is situated in the castle stables. You may be so enamoured of Kilkenny that you choose to stay the night here and continue exploring tomorrow. If so, consider taking a detour north along the N78 to see the **Dunmore Cave** near Mohill, (daily, hours vary). First mentioned in 9th-century Irish *triads* (the arrangement of ideas in groups of three), this limestone cave was the site of a Viking massacre in 928.

If you decide to continue, your route back to Waterford takes you first on the R697 southward to **Kells**, not to be confused with the Kells in County Meath, where the famous *Book of Kells* manuscript was found.

Kells

The first sight of the town from afar is one of the great surprises of Ireland. It seems we behold not a religious centre but a mighty battlemented citadel with towers as awesome as the Rock of Cashel. The massive walls hide 2 hectares (5 acres) of ruined priory.

Our final destination is **Jerpoint Abbey** (Mar–Nov daily; Dec–Mar open for group bookings; tel 056-24623), which lies east, beyond Stonyford. Do not miss this abbey. It was founded in 1158 by the Cistercians and is one of the finest and mightiest of monastic ruins in Ireland. Here, among the cloisters, the quadrangle and the three-naved church with its Romanesque arches, you can easily picture the might of the Church in its heyday. The cloisters are particularly fine and there are many interesting carvings and effigies. Turning left from Jerpoint we join the N9 southbound and, in just over 30 minutes, return to Waterford.

Above: sculpture at Jerpoint Abbey

17. WATERFORD TO WEXFORD *(see map p62)*

This tour starts with Waterford city and a coastal drive to Hook Head to see Europe's oldest lighthouse. It continues to the enchanting anchorage at Slade; Tintern Abbey ruins and Kilmore Quay; and visits the Irish National Heritage Park, Ferrycarrig, before reaching Wexford.

Begin at **Waterford**'s award-winning **Museum of Treasures** at the Granary, Merchants Quay. Here you can explore the 1,000-year history of Ireland's oldest city (daily year-round). The celebrated crystal factory is situated at **Kilbarry** to the southeast of the centre and offers a guided tour and audio-visual presentation. The city, at the mouth of the River Suir, has two cathedrals and has played a major role in history. Founded by the Danes, it was the first stronghold that fell to the Anglo-Norman invasion of 1170, an event that would slowly break up old Celtic Ireland and bring about 700 years of turmoil. Worth seeing are the cathedrals of Christ Church and Holy Trinity, as well as **Reginald's Tower** *(see page 61 for opening hours)*. Built in the 12th century on a Viking site, it formed part of the town's defences, and at different times in its history has been a mint, a prison and a military store. Today it houses an exhibition.

Around Waterford

Departing from Waterford, take the well-signed road to **Passage East** to cross the swift-running estuary of Waterford Harbour by ferry. It was here that the Norman invader, Strongbow, landed with his fighting force in 1170, to be joined a year later by Henry II of England. The ferry runs every 15 minutes (up to 8pm in winter, 10pm in summer), and delivers you at **Arthurstown**, with its anchorages for small fishing boats. Nearby is Dunbrody Park, the family seat of the Marquess of Donegal, and **Dunbrody Abbey** and visitors centre (May–June and Sept, 10am–6pm; July–Aug, 10am–7pm). This Cistercian abbey was founded in 1210. Nearby, the ruins of Dunbrody Castle house a craft shop and there is a full-size hedge maze – one of only two in Ireland. A little further north is the **John F Kennedy Arboretum and Visitor Centre** (May–Aug 10am–8pm; closes 6.30pm Apr & Sept, 5pm Oct–Mar) created as a memorial since the family originally came from nearby Dunganstown . Around 4,500 types of trees and shrubs, donated by many nations, cover the slopes of Slieve Caoilte, a rebel battle camp in 1798.

On the way back to Arthurstown, follow the signs to **Ballyhack**, a quaint village, for lunch at the Neptune Restaurant, specialising in seafood. The castle, a 15th-century tower house, has a good view of the Waterford estuary and houses several heritage exhibitions (Jun–Sept daily).

Back in Arthurstown, follow the east side of Waterford Harbour until the road heads inland, then turn right to pick up the road signs for Hook Head.

Right: chandeliers of famous Waterford crystal

The drive for the next 16km (10 miles) has fine coastal views across the broad estuary. The lighthouse standing at **Hook Head** is reputedly Europe's oldest surviving lighthouse, dating to the early 13th century. Beneath its bulky Norman tower are cells once inhabited by the monks who manned the early beacon. It has been renovated to provide an interpretive centre and craft shop (Mar–Oct 9.30am–5.30pm; tel: 051-397055 for details).

Castles and Tintern Abbey

For far more spectacular views, cross the pencil-thin peninsula to **Slade**, a detour of less than 2km (1¼ miles), before returning. Just go straight on and do not turn left. This must be the most enchanting fishing harbour in all of Ireland, from which rises a deserted castle built by the Laffan family in the 17th century. You can have a look inside if you like. The key is available from the caretaker, who lives nearby.

Return on the same road that came up the peninsula, but turn right to **Fethard**, a busy summer resort, with Baginbun Head where Strongbow's scouting force landed. The area around Fethard is rich in early church and castle ruins. Some 8km (5 miles) further along is the awesome Cistercian **Tintern Abbey**, founded by William the Earl Marshall in 1200 to honour his vow of thanks for surviving a stormy crossing from England after his boat beached in the nearby creek (mid-June–Sept, 9.30am–6.30pm; tel 051-562650 for winter opening times; guided tours available on request). Turn right off the R734 and take the R733 to Wellington Bridge. Looking south from the bridge a castle can be seen among the ruins of **Clonmines**, a silver mining town that died in the 17th century after the river silted up.

The next stop is **Kilmore Quay**, famous for its thatched cottages, some 20km (12½ miles) down the R736. Kilmore Quay is the departure point for boat outings to the bird sanctuaries on the Saltee Islands. Sadly, the thatched cottages are drowning among the modern developments that are springing up all around them. Next, turn inland to **Kilmore**. On the far side of the vil-

Above: Slade Harbour

lage, just before the cemetery on the right, is a hawthorn tree. Among the branches are piles of funeral crosses. Following ancient custom, two funeral crosses accompany the deceased and one is placed in the tree. The origin of this strange practice is unclear. Some 6km (3¾ miles) north of Kilmore you can turn right onto the R736 and seek out the Tacumshin Windmill, or continue towards Wexford on the R739. To the left will be signed **Rathmacknee Castle**, seat of the Rossiter family and now a ruin. You can get the key from the family who live within the castle precincts. Take care if walking around

the roof as no guard rails exist. Perhaps the best reason for visiting is to meet the family who have a castle surrounding their home. County Wexford has many examples like this of homes sprouting from within castle ruins.

Proceed not into Wexford but on, via the bypass, to **Johnstown Castle**, a Gothic Revival fantasy. Its mature shrub gardens, an arboretum and ornamental lakes are open to the public. **The Irish Agricultural Museum and Famine Exhibition** (June–Aug, daily; Apr–May and Sept–Oct, closed am weekends; Nov–Mar weekdays only), is within the castle grounds. On leaving, turn left and follow the signs for the **Irish National Heritage Park** at Ferrycarrig (daily 9.30am–6.30pm; tel: 053-20733 to confirm winter closing times). This is a well thought-out project, which portrays human evolution from 7000BC to the 12th century. Accurate reconstructions have been made by archaeologists, based on information from excavated sites. The tableaux, which you can either explore independently or with a guide (1½ hours), will tell you all about dolmens, stone circles, ring forts, Celtic villages and vanished lifestyles.

Wexford

Finally, you reach **Wexford**, former home of Commodore John Barry, founder of the US Navy. The streets are so amazingly narrow that parking is practically impossible. The **Westgate Heritage Centre** (tel: 053-46506 for opening times) in the restored Westgate Tower of the old medieval wall has an audio-visual display on the history of Wexford town. This is the end point of your journey round Ireland's coast.

As a last reminder of all that is wild and beautiful about Ireland, head out at sunset across the harbour bridge and take the road to North Slob. This road leads to the **Wildfowl Protection Area**, where innumerable birds gather, mainly Greenland white-fronted geese. At times, especially winter evenings, they take off *en masse* and darken the sky, creating an awesome sight, which can best be enjoyed from the observation tower.

Above: Irish National Heritage Park
Right: Hook Head lighthouse

Leisure Activities

SHOPPING

Dublin

The first rule of the shopper says 'start at the top of the hill when empty-handed'. **Grafton Street**, one of Dublin's two main shopping thoroughfares, is on an incline rising from College Green, so starting at the **St Stephen's Green Shopping Centre** at the top of Grafton Street would seem sensible. In this gracious, glass-roofed complex are some 75 shops ranging from fashion and designer wear to Irish crafts. The sweeter-toothed might prefer to start at **Butler's Handmade Chocolate** shop right opposite.

Some 50m (150ft) down Grafton Street turn left towards the **Powerscourt Townhouse** complex. It occupies the courtyard of a restored Georgian townhouse and offers entertainment and live music, antiques, Irish handmade goods including Celtic jewellery, crystal and designer clothes as well as several restaurants. For the best of Irish fashion visit the **Design Centre**, where you have a choice of clothes by designers such as Louise Kennedy and Mariad Whisker. If you feel like a bite to eat, you can pop into **Chompeys**, an American deli.

Before returning to Grafton Street look for **Magill's Deli** on nearby Clarendon Street, which sells all manner of Irish produce such as preserves, jams, honey, smoked foods and cheeses. Back on Grafton Street visit **A-Wear**, a fashion store selling cut-price designer clothes, including John Rocha and Quin and Donnelly collections. At the lower end of Grafton Street are **Brown Thomas** and **Arnott's** department stores offering leading fashions. If you need a break, stop for coffee at **Bewley's Oriental Café**, halfway up Grafton Street, whose coffee-roasting aromas attract everyone who passes by. Since 1840 the mahogany-panelled rooms have wrapped themselves round politicians, students, po-

ets and artists who mingle with out-of-town shoppers. Before leaving, buy a coffee or chocolates to take home. Bewleys also have shop-restaurants on Mary Street and Westmoreland Street.

Turning right into busy **Nassau Street** you will find speciality shops for Donegal tweeds, Aran sweaters, Royal Tara chinaware and Irish pewter. Here Kevin and Howlin stock quality Irish woollens and tweeds, as do the **Blarney Woollen Mills**. It's worth noting, though, that the Dublin Woollen Mills on the north side of the Ha'penny Bridge also stock woollen goods and often at more bargain prices.

Almost next door to the Blarney Woollen Mills is the **Kilkenny Shop** presenting an array of Irish arts and crafts including fabrics, candles, pottery, glass and woodwork. They also have a selection of Irish-made preserves and confectionery and on the first floor there is an excellent self-service restaurant overlooking the Trinity College playing fields. On the same

Left: colourful crafts
Right: Waterford glass at the Kilkenny Shop

Square. Off the Square in Essex Street you'll find the **DESIGNyard** Jewellery Gallery, which promotes and sells Irish and European works in both precious and non-precious materials. Upstair the Crafts Council **DESIGN**yard exhibits and sells Irish-designed and manufactured textiles, leather goods, pottery, lighting and furniture. **WhichCraft** on Cows Lane showcases the best in contemporary Irish crafts, jewellery, pottery and furnishings. Fishing enthusiasts can talk to the experts in **Rory's Fishing Tackle**.

If you are looking to buy something off-beat in art or antiques it is worth making a diversion to **Thomas Street**, a seedy but rewarding area beyond Christchurch Cathedral. Dublin's antiques trade mainly centres on Francis Street in the Liberties but there are a number of other traders scattered about the city, especially in the small streets off Grafton Street and around the Liffey quays.

North of the Liffey, the **Henry Street** area, off O'Connell Street, is the other main shopping centre of the city. Here you will find wall-to-wall boutiques, shoe shops, Roches, Arnotts and Dunnes department stores and the **ILAC Centre**, which has many small clothes shops, and several eateries and coffee shops. Off Henry Street is the **Moore Street Market**, a noisy free-for-all, with traders buying and selling everything imaginable. Illegal traders ply their wares up and down the length of Henry Street, especially at Christmas time, with a keen eye out for the 'boys in blue'. At the far end of Henry Street is the **Jervis Street Shopping Centre**, dominated by British chainstores.

If you are planning to explore the great outdoors on this trip, you will find camping shops further along Mary Street and down Capel Street, which will help kit you out for a very reasonable price. If you've come this far you'll be in dire need of a reviving cup of coffee and Bewley's in Mary Street will be happy to provide you with one.

Rural Ireland

Driving from town to town you will find craft centres, hardware stores and even family homes selling **traditional loom-woven**

street the **Celtic Note** shop specialises in Irish music. If you have Irish family connections, the genealogy shop of **Heraldic Artists** is the place to trace your lineage. Lovers of cheese will find their heart's desire in nearby Trinity Street at the **Big Cheese Company**, which has an excellent selection of Irish-made cheeses.

Bibliophiles can spend many happy hours browsing in Dublin's numerous bookshops, such as **Hodges Figgis**, established in the 18th century, which faces **Waterstone's**, part of the British chain, across Dawson Street. **Fred Hanna**, around the corner in Nassau Street, has catered for generations of students at Trinity College (across the road). If your interests lie in rare or antiquarian works then a visit to **Cathach Books** in Duke Street is a must. The **Winding Stair**, on the Lower Ormond Quay, near the Ha'penny Bridge is also strong on rare books and the self-service restaurant on the first floor serves inexpensive tasty meals.

Temple Bar is another place where the book-lover can browse contentedly. An open-air market is held there every Saturday during the summer months in Meeting

Above: Schull sweaters

tweeds. Even in the middle of nowhere you can often find that 'special something', particularly in the west and south. All **country market towns** have excellent shops offering woodwork, linens, lace, plaids, books, prints, crystal, ornaments and jewellery.

Special items

Antiques

Though no longer the bargains they once were, Irish furniture, sterling silver items and Irish landscape paintings can still be found. In Dublin, try the Francis Street area *(see Dublin Shopping)*.

Marble

Connemara marble and other colourful stone, fashioned into everything from book-ends to cheeseboards, is on sale throughout the country.

Pottery & Fine China

Throughout Ireland studio pottery is thriving. The famous Belleek bone china is sold in department stores everywhere.

Art

Dublin galleries are as adventurous as the new young artists who exhibit in them. Fine traditional watercolour landscapes can be found across the land.

Crystal & Glassware

World-famous Waterford crystal is sold all over Ireland, but crystal from Tipperary, Galway and Dublin is becoming popular, and is challenging the Waterford monopoly.

Tweed

Hand-woven tweeds from rural Ireland are renowned worldwide for their quality, design, versatility and rich colour blends. In the west, most tweeds are still woven on looms in the home. You can buy directly from the weaver, or be less adventurous and buy at sales centres such as Magee's in Donegal.

Music

The recent popularity of Irish traditional music has resulted in the appearance of stores selling everything from recordings, music and song sheets to the instruments themselves, though these are of varying quality.

For the Home Bar & Larder

Whiskey (spelled with an 'e' to distinguish it from Scotch whisky) makes an excellent present. Smoked salmon, cheeses, bacon and conserves are also popular. In Dublin visit the Old Jameson Distillery (Bow Street, Smithfield, tel: 01-807 2355). Near Cork, visit the Jameson Heritage Centre at Midleton (tel: 021-461 3594). It is worth trailing through the mills because at the end you get to sample the whiskey.

Jewellery

Celtic traditions live on, and craft centres stock items ranging from repro ancient Celtic gold, silver and enamel work to daring contemporary designs, and all styles in between.

Linen and Lace

Look out for fine table coverings, furnishing fabrics, shirts and blouses as well as smaller items such as handkerchiefs.

Handknits

Aran Island sweaters, scarves, caps, gloves, etc, are made from undyed wool to family patterns passed down for generations. Donegal and nearby Ardara have the best range, but you can also buy them at Blarney Woollen Mills throughout the country.

Right: St Columb's House Kitchen

EATING OUT

Ireland was until fairly recently an agricultural country, and early mornings combined with long days of hard manual labour call for **substantial fare** to rekindle the inner fire. Irish food, traditionally, has been plain but hearty and plentiful. Bread, potatoes and root vegetables have served to eke out and soak up the meat and juices of stew cooked slowly in a tureen over an open peat fire. Such traditional fare is still to be found in the home and in rural hotel dining rooms, but a new generation of gifted chefs, have transformed the 'poor man's' food of Ireland into dishes fit for earls and kings.

Irish cooking is no longer a 'bacon and cabbage' cuisine, but one reliant on quality produce, especially beef, lamb, farmhouse cheeses and Atlantic Coast fish and shellfish. **Irish stew**, for example, can be a heavy dish of mutton, potatoes and onions but, in the hands of a gifted chef who uses the best cuts of lamb and herb-fragrant stock, it can be a superbly light and flavoursome dish. In Dublin, Kinsale and Galway, in particular, you will find no shortage of gourmet experiences, although you may find prices a bit steep, while country house hotels often provide excellent food in beautiful surroundings. Many pubs provide tasty filling meals and represent very good value for money.

Breakfasts in Ireland are still hearty enough to fuel you for the day. Expect a gargantuan plate of fried bacon, sausage, eggs and tomatoes as just one course of the first meal of the day, sometimes accompanied by black pudding and **savoury potato cakes**. If you indulge in breakfast to the full, you may only want a light lunch; most pubs serve bar food ranging from sandwiches and salads to more substantial roasts and stews. *Boxties*, traditional stuffed pancakes, can be found on many regional menus.

Travelling in the west of Ireland you will encounter numerous restaurants specialising in fish, freshly caught and of the highest quality. Salmon, river trout and oysters are commonplace luxuries that make eating here both pleasurable and healthy. Mussels, crab and lobster are also popular. Do not be surprised if, among the traditional Irish bars and restaurants, you also find Chinese restaurants serving some of the best and most **authentic fish dishes** to be found outside Asia itself.

Game will also feature on the menu if you are travelling in the autumn and winter. Dishes of venison, pheasant, quail, duck, woodcock and rabbit are all likely to appear on the menu, along with the all-season staples such as steak, lamb and pork. Irish **beef and lamb** are considered among the best in the world, with east-coast lamb praised for its delicacy and Connemara lamb enjoyed for its intensity and herb flavourings.

Outside cities and major tourist centres, there is still a tendency to **eat early**; until comparatively recently, lack of electricity for lighting in rural areas meant that you went to bed with the sun.

Outside the big cities, **dairy products** play an important role in Irish cuisine. Homemade or farmhouse cheeses, such as Cashel Blue, a soft, creamy blue cheese, are fast becoming known. **Bread** in most good restaurants tends to be delicious and home-made, with soda bread the most typical. Irish bread goes very well with the simple farmhouse cheeses from the Midlands or County Cork. Irish **fruit** tends to be fairly limited but the quality of soft fruits, in particular, is very good. County Wexford is usually considered the centre of the soft fruit industry and is noted for its magnificent strawberries. In short, the view of Ireland as a centre of a 'bacon and cabbage' cuisine is no longer deserved. Restaurants will be busiest between 7.30pm and 8.30pm, so consider booking ahead if you plan to eat at this time.

RESTAURANTS
Dublin City

For Dubliners, dining in a restaurant is an occasion; and the design and décor of the surroundings, the clientele and the whole atmosphere are just as important as the food. In this small city, restaurants tend to be distinctive. As in most capitals, the top of the market is dominated by the French interpretations, but in Dublin all cuisine has its own special character due to the freshness and purity of the ingredients available here. Fish is landed and eaten on the same day. The very quality of all the 'raw' foods presents a persistent incentive and challenge to chefs. This has helped stamp a distinctively Irish culinary individuality – even 'sushi' is Irish when it is sliced from a locally caught salmon! Dublin now offers such cosmopolitan cuisine as Pacific Rim and Provençal, Chinese and cajun, with American and Italian influences predominating. The ratings in this guide refer to a meal for two excluding wine. Meals can vary in price from €12 to €250-plus, depending on your taste and your pocket:

€€€ = Expensive (over €80)
€€ = Moderate (€50–€80)
€ = Inexpensive (under €50)

Citron
Fitzwilliam Hotel, St Stephen's Green, Dublin 2
Tel: 01-478 7000. €€€
The place for those who like celebrity spotting, lemon-lime theme decor, and modern European cuisine.

Cornucopia
19 Wicklow Street, Dublin 2
Tel: 01-677 7583. €
Popular vegetarian restaurant, with terrific soups for a cold day, among other tasty offerings.

L'Ecrivain
190A Lower Baggot Street, Dublin 2
Tel: 01-661 1919. €€
Delicious French-inspired food. Very popular, so you need to book ahead.

King Sitric
Howth
Tel: 01-832 2624. €€
Family owned restaurant on the tip of Howth Peninsula. The exquisite seafood dishes are definitely worth the trip and there are four guest rooms available if you investigate the wine list too thoroughly.

Lock's
1 Windsor Terrace, Dublin 8
Tel: 01-454 3391. €€€
This is where the well-heeled and well-known come to dine in discreet elegance. Excellent food and extensive wine list.

Mona Lisa
D'Olier Chambers
16A D'Olier Street, Dublin 2
Tel: 01-677 0499. €
Italian food. Happy hour 4.30–6.30pm – half-price pizzas and pastas. Good for lunch.

Nico's
53 Dame Street, Dublin 2
Tel: 01-677 3062. €€
Old-fashioned romantic restaurant, with tasty Italian dishes served by the soft glow of candlelight.

Rajdoot Tandoori
26 Clarendon Street, Dublin 2
Tel: 01-679 4274. €€
High-quality tandoori dishes in the restaurant that set the standard for Indian cuisine in Dublin.

Restaurant Patrick Guilbaud
21 Upper Merrion Street, Dublin 2
Tel: 01-661 0052. €€€ ++

Dublin's most serious French restaurant, with a Michelin one-star rating. The highly professional, innovative kitchen is known for turning the finest of Ireland's 'freshest' into art. Their gastronomic Menu Surprise consists of six courses and is created individually for each table. Prices are commensurately high and way above the ratings given.

The Tea Room
Clarence Hotel
Wellington Quay, Dublin 2
Tel: 01-670 7766. €€€
Gastronomic cuisine (not afternoon tea!) in the Art Nouveau ballroom of U2's Clarence Hotel; food ranges from Pacific Rim to Italian, and has won the Becks Taste of Temple Bar Award for its excellent quality.

The Northwest
Donegal
Harvey's Point
Lough Eske, Donegal, Co Donegal
Tel: 074-9722208. €€€
Smart-casual dress for this high-quality restaurant serving French and Irish cuisine.

Nesbitt Arms Hotel
Adara, Co Donegal
Tel: . €
Good quality pub dishes with daily specials featuring local seafood.

County Sligo
The Embassy Restaurant
JFK Parade, Sligo, Co Sligo
Tel: 071-9161250. €€
'New' Irish cuisine, served on the waterfront overlooking the Garavogue River. Well worth a stop for its healthy, 'natural' food, efficiently served.

The Far West
Newport
Newport House & Restaurant
Newport, Co Mayo
Tel: 098-41222. €€
Five-course meals inventively prepared using excellent local freshwater fish and seafood caught off nearby Achill Island. Their walled garden provides fresh vegetables as accompaniment. Very good wine list.

Westport
Ardmore Country House & Restaurant
The Quay, Westport, Co Mayo
Tel: 098-25994. €€
Family-run restaurant serving locally caught seafood and game.

Quay Cottage
The Quay, Westport, Co Mayo
Tel: 098-26412. €€
Lively and informal bar decorated with fishing tackle, and a seafood restaurant of excellent quality.

County Galway
Galway
Conlon's Seafood Restaurant
3 Eglinton Court, Galway, Co Galway.
Tel: 091-561063. €€
Inexpensive. Very fresh fish and oysters.

The River God Café
2 High Street, Galway, Co Galway
Tel: 091-565811. €
International and French cuisine prepared by three French chefs. Lunch on Friday and Saturday only.

GBC Restaurant
7 Williamsgate Street, Galway
Co Galway
Tel: 091-563087. €
Welcoming restaurant in a period house. Seafood, poultry and vegetarian cuisine.

Clifden
Abbeyglen Castle Hotel
Sky Road, Clifden, Co Galway
Tel: 095-21201. €€
Gourmet cuisine, especially oysters and lobster. Piano playing; views of Clifden.

D'Arcy Inn
Main Street, Clifden, Co Galway
Tel: 095-21146. €
Seafood and lobsters in profusion at a reasonable price.

E.J. King's Bar and Restaurant
The Square, Clifden, Co Galway
Tel: 095-21330. €€
Friendly service and tasty fresh food, which is locally produced.

County Limerick
Limerick
Brulées Restaurant
Corner of Henry Street and Mallow Street
Limerick
Tel: 061-319 931. €€
Limerick's shining light of fine dining, serving modern Irish cooking with the freshest of ingredients. Many veggy options.

Freddy's Bistro
Glentworth Street, Limerick
Tel: 061-418749. €€
Award-winning friendly, family-run restaurant. Good Irish food.

Mustard Seed At Echo Lodge
Balingarry (near Adare)
Co Limerick
Tel: 069-68508. €€€
Modern gourmet Irish cuisine in an 1880s country house overlooking the village of Ballingary. Accommodation is provided too. Enjoy afternoon tea by log fires after a day's fishing, horse riding, cycling, walking or golf, all available in the surrounding area.

County Kerry
Dingle
Beginish Restaurant
Green Street, Dingle, Co Kerry
Tel: 066-9151588. €€
Small, elegant townhouse. Outstanding, lightly sauced seafood dishes with fresh catch, along with a choice of meat or fowl.

Killarney
Dingles
New Street, Killarney, Co Kerry
Tel: 064-31079. €€
This cosy front-parlour restaurant is in an old townhouse and features fresh local produce prepared in traditional ways on the pan or grill. Open fire. Closed Tues. No lunch.

Gaby's Seafood Restaurant
27 High Street, Killarney, Co Kerry
Tel: 064-32519. €€
One of Ireland's oldest seafood restaurants, in the centre of town; fresh seafood; informal atmosphere.

County Cork
Cork
Eastern Tandoori
1–2 Emmet Place, Cork, Co Cork
Tel: 021-4272020. €
As a change from other cuisines, sample one of the best Indian restaurants in Ireland, rated in the Top 100 Indian Restaurants in Europe in the *Good Curry Guide.*

Bantry
O'Connor's Seafood Bar and Restaurant
Wolfe Tone Square, Bantry, Co Cork
Tel: 027-50221. €

Family-owned bar-restaurant serving bay mussels, live lobster, seafood and steaks.

Kinsale
The Blue Haven
3 Pearse Street, Kinsale, Co Cork
Tel: 021-4772209. €€
Outstanding seafood served in a charming setting, with a conservatory and garden.

Cottage Loft
6 Main Street, Kinsale, Co Cork
Tel: 021-4772803. €
Gourmet cuisine from a gifted local owner/ chef. Seafood in a low-key but charming setting. (Guest-house accommodation.)

Crackpots
Kinsale, Co Cork
Tel:. €€€
Fantastic seafood dishes and a good selection for vegetarians too. The pottery shop nextdoor supplies the plates you eat from.

Kieran's Folkhouse Inn
Guardwell, Kinsale, Co Cork
Tel: 021-4772382. €€
Snug seafaring inn, with a small hotel, cosy bars and a restaurant with inventive dishes.

Youghal
Molana Restaurant
Devonshire Arms Hotel
Pearse Square, Youghal, Co Cork
Tel: 024-92827. €€
Classic gourmet cuisine and bistro. Reservations only during off-season.

Waterford City
Dwyer's
8 Mary Street
Waterford, Co Waterford
Tel: 051-332575. €€
A great restaurant in the middle of one of the area's most interesting towns. Self-service, but hearty food made from the best of local produce. Children welcome.

Gatchell's
Waterford Crystal Visitor Centre, Kilbarry
Waterford, Co Waterford
Tel: 051-877478. €€
In the town centre; imaginative dishes in a cosily converted police barracks.

The Wine Vault
High Street
Waterford, Co Waterford
Tel: 051-853444. €€
Informal bistro-style cooking. Seafood, steak, chicken, and game in season.

Kilkenny City
Rinuccini Restaurant
The Parade, Kilkenny, Co Kilkenny
Tel: 056-7761575. €€
The city's best restaurant serves both Irish and Italian cuisine .

Café Sol
William Street, Kilkenny, Co Kilkenny
Tel: 056-7764987. €
Cheap and cheerful café-style restauran situatedt opposite the town hall. Home cooking: warm salads, fresh pasta and fish of the day.

Lacken House
Dublin Road, Kilkenny, Co Kilkenny
Tel: 056-7761085. €€
Restaurant situated in genteel old Georgian cellar, serving freshly prepared food using seasonal local ingredients.

Above: fresh produce

NIGHTLIFE

Dublin

The Dublin pub has a long tradition of being the informal meeting ground of mind with mind, the exchange of wit and humour and the sanctuary for talkers (though no longer smokers). Although many of the old bars have changed their décor, some keep alive the ghosts of Dublin's past. The way to visit them is by selecting an area that has pubs of special character, after first having a 'ritual' drink in the **Horseshoe Bar** in the **Shelbourne Hotel** on St Stephen's Green.

On Lower Baggot Street, less than a minute's walk from St Stephen's Green, is **O'Donoghue's**, famous for its traditional music and the place where *The Dubliners* first began their career. Hardly a minute beyond is **Doheny and Nesbitt** with its 'snug' set around a mahogany bar below a smoke-encrusted ceiling; a favourite meeting place of writers, raconteurs and journalists. Opposite, **Toner's**, with its wooden storage drawers, dates back to the early 19th century.

Working your way up Grafton Street, sampling the bars, is an enjoyable way to spend the evening. Starting from the Nassau Street end, the first stop on the left is **Kehoe's** in South Anne Street, with its finely carved confessional partitions. Next is the **Bailey** in Duke Street, where Gogarty is supposed to have introduced James Joyce to the pleasure of drink. It serves excellent roasts and oak-smoked salmon upstairs.

Nearby in Duke Street is another Joycean pub: **Davy Byrne's** 'moral pub' is featured in *Ulysses* and is noted for its good food. On the other side of Grafton Street is **Neary's** in Chatham Street, noticeable by its lanterns and Edwardian atmosphere.

Another group of pubs, concentrated in the Trinity College area, are also full of character. **Bowes**, in Fleet Street, is all mirrors and mahogany and is a favourite haunt of journalists. The **Palace Bar**, also in Fleet Street, is where hacks from the *Irish Times* gather to relax. For real native Dubliners, **Mulligan's** in Poolbeg Street beats them all.

If you like to be entertained while you drink, then **Murphy's Laughter Lounge** at O'Connell Bridge is for you. Every Thursday, Friday and Saturday night Irish and international stand-up comedians perform.

Theatres

Dublin has a long theatrical tradition stretching all the way back to Georgian times, though it was not until the turn of the 20th century that Irish writers were able to break away from outside influences and find their own voice. Today, Dublin's theatres play an important role in Irish cultural life.

**The National Theatre
(The Abbey and Peacock theatres)**
Lower Abbey Street
Tel: 01-8872200
Founded by Yeats and Lady Gregory. Specialises in works by Irish playwrights.

Above: a night out in Temple Bar

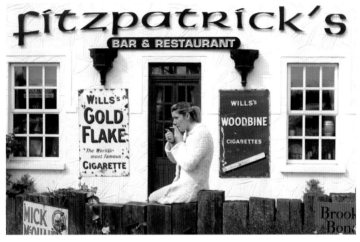

The Gaiety Theatre
119 St Stephens Green
Tel: 01-6771717
Productions reflective of Broadway and London's West End. Has two opera seasons.

The Gate Theatre
1 Cavendish Row
Tel: 01-8744045
Classic Irish productions, plus European notables such as Ibsen and Chekov. Orson Welles made his first stage appearance here.

Traditional Music
Music lovers worldwide are awakening to the intoxicating sound of Irish traditional music. A gathering of musicians, always on an informal basis, is known as a *seisiún* (session) and can be best compared to animated conversation, sometimes casual but often passionate. A good *seisiún* is to be experienced rather than described. Many of the best places for traditional music are within 15 minutes' walk of the city centre, but it's a good idea to call before turning up as venues and events are liable to change at short notice:

The Brazen Head
20 Lower Bridge Street
Tel: 01-6795186
Music is played most nights of the week in the atmospheric confines of the 'oldest bar in Dublin', in what was once the Viking area of the city.

Hughes Pub
19 Chancery Street
Tel: 01-8726540
Traditional music from 9.30pm nightly.

O'Shea's Merchant Pub
12 Lower Bridge Street,
Tel: 01-6793797
Music and set dancing most nights, 9.30pm.

Abbey Tavern
Howth, Co Dublin
Tel: 01-8390307
Traditional Irish music on Sat/Sun at 9pm with the Abbey Singers. Dancers in high season. Booking essential.

Irish Traditional Music Archive
63 Merton Square South
Tel: 01-6619699
A repository of traditional music – for the serious enthusiast.

The Nightclub Scene
Dublin is a hive of nocturnal activity and has an immensely lively club scene, catering for every type of night-owl. Most of the clubs are situated close to the city centre and provide a range of haunts for the trendy and sophisticated.

As a rule, the club scene is divided into fully licensed clubs serving a full range of drinks, with a cover charge of about €10–15; and wine-only clubs with no cover fee. Both have strict door policies and expensive

Above: the smoking ban in the Republic's pubs and restaurants drives smokers outdoors

drinks. Generally a pint of lager will cost about €5, with €25–35 being the average for a bottle of wine. To keep up with the nightclub scene, check venues in the bi-monthly *In Dublin* magazine.

Lillie's Bordello
Adam Court (off Grafton Street),
Tel: 01-6799204
A sought-after spot for supermodels and rock stars. This boudoir-style club is selective so come in your best bib and tucker..

The Kitchen
Clarence Hotel, Wellington Quay
Tel: 01-6776635
Trendy young club in U2-owned hotel.

Reynard's
35–37 South Frederick Street
Tel: 01-6775876
Another magnet for the trendy.

Spy Club
Powerscourt Townhouse Centre, Dublin 2
Tel: 01-6770014
Favourite haunt for well-known faces.

The Leeson Street Strip
'The Strip' consists of half a dozen small underground nightclubs which run the length of Leeson Street. They serve only wines and have no cover charge. These subterranean dens operate midnight–dawn, and can be identified by black-suited bouncers outside.

POD
35 Old Harcourt Street
Tel: 01-4780225
Set in an old railway vault, the **Place of Dance** appeals to dance fanatics.

Rural Ireland
'Impromptu' is the keyword for all nightlife in country towns and villages. An evening out usually means visiting a pub for live traditional music. There is no set programme – activities 'happen'. If you are a musician yourself, take along your instrument.

There are several good regional theatres and cultural centres in the larger towns, such as Cork, Limerick, Galway, Wexford and Kilkenny. Several less well-known towns,

including Tralee and Cashel, run reputable folk theatres. (In Tralee, contact the Siamsa Tíre Company; tel: 066-7123055). The Shannon Development Corporation's medieval banquets are well worth attending (tel: 061-361555). Expect jesters, folk dances, 'medieval' food – and lots of blarney.

However, the best nightlife is to be found in the pubs. Here are a few typical pubs; you'll find others in the itineraries.

Kytelers
Kieren Street, Kilkenny, Co Kilkenny
Tel: 056-7721064
This inn was the house of Alice Kyteler, who was accused of witchcraft and died in 1324. The cellar bar is darkly atmospheric.

Durty Nellie's Pub
Bunratty, Co Limerick
Tel: 061-77364072
This boisterous and welcoming inn dates back to 1620. An enjoyable prelude to the banquet next door at Bunratty Castle.

Reginald's Bar Tavern
Beside Reginald's Tower
Waterford, Co Waterford
Tel: 051-855087
Set beside the Viking bastion, this long-established pub and restaurant adjoins the ancient city wall.

1601
Pearce Street, Kinsale, Co Cork
Tel: 021-4772529
This popular pub was named after the decisive Battle of Kinsale in 1601, which marked the end of the old Gaelic order. Inside, however, the Celtic spirit is very much alive, as is the *craic*.

Right: a pint of best Guinness

CALENDAR OF EVENTS

January–February

Point-to-point horseracing season begins. Races are held all over Ireland, usually on a Sunday.

The Six Nations rugby season begins, with matches at Lansdowne Road, Dublin.

ESAT **Young Scientists and Technology Exhibition**, in the RDS Ballsbridge, Dublin. Young scientists from all over the country compete against each other for the coveted title. January.

Oireachtas Rince na hEireann (All-Ireland Dancing Championships) are held in different venues throughout the country. Solo and team events. February.

March–May

All Ireland Drama Festival is held at various venues. Drama groups from all over Ireland compete. May.

Irish Master's Snooker Tournament, draws the leading lights in international snooker. Citywest Hotel, Saggart, Co Dublin. March.

Cork International Choral Festival is held at various venues throughout the city of Cork. May.

Cat Laughs Comedy Festival is five days of fun and lunacy with performances by top comedians from Ireland, the UK and America. Kilkenny. May/June.

Dublin Film Festival exhibits the best in Irish and International cinema at various cinemas throughout Dublin. April.

A Feis Ceoil is held in various venues throughout Dublin. Competitive music festival for voice and instruments. March.

Kerry Arts Festival is held at participating venues in Kerry. March/April.

Kinsale International Point-to-Point Festival is a two-day end-of-season National Hunt point-to-point held in Killagh, Kinsale, Co Cork. It is tough enough to test the most skilled horsemanship. May.

St Patrick's Day witnesses celebrations all over Ireland for the feast of the nation's patron saint, including street parades in Dublin and traditional music festivals all over the country. Should the festival fall on a weekend, the following Monday will be a bank holiday. 17 March.

West of Ireland Amateur Open Championships is a must for golfing enthusiasts. Enniscore, Co Sligo. April.

The Irish Grand National horse-race takes place at Fairyhouse, Co Meath. Easter.

County Wicklow Gardens Festival, with gardens and gourmet cuisine. May–July.

The Irish 2,000 Guineas horse-race takes place at the Curragh, Co Kildare. May.

Mussel Festival is a feast for the tastebuds. Bantry. May.

Sligo Arts Week. May/June.

June–August

Bloomsday Literary Festival is a celebration of the author James Joyce. It is staged in Dublin with a pilgrimage around the city visiting all the places mentioned in *Ulysses*, as well as readings from the writer's landmark novel. 16 June.

Ballyjamesduff International Pork Festival is held at Ballyjamesduff in Co Cavan. Open-air barbecue, live music and lots more. June.

Bathmullen Fishing Festival lights up this small town in Co Donegal. June.

Éigse Carlow Arts Festival is celebrated at various venues in Carlow town. Street theatre, music, dance and art exhibitions are among the attractions. June.

County Wexford Strawberry Fair at Enniscorthy, Co Wexford. July.

Murphy's Irish Open: international golf. Held at different venues. Early July.

The Salthill Air Show is a display of spectacular aerobatics at Salthill, Co Galway. July.

Woman's Mini Marathon, Dublin. June.

Yeats International Summer School, Yeats Memorial Building, Hawk's Well Theatre, Sligo. Lectures, seminars, poetry readings and tours. July/Aug.

The Festival of Music in Great Irish Houses, classical concerts in stately homes around Dublin. June.

The Irish Derby takes place at the Curragh, Co Kildare. June.

The Dublin Horse Show stages a mixture of horsey events for both professionals and amateurs at the Showgrounds, RDS Ballsbridge, Dublin. It's one of the social events of the year, and a place where the fashionable like to be seen. August.

Listowel Writers' Week, a fascinating literary festival, is a chance to hear Irish writers read their works. Co Cork. May/June.

Lough Derg Pilgrimage sees pilgrims travelling in vast numbers to pray on Holy Island, a monastic site on Lough Derg. June–mid-August.

Croagh Patrick Pilgrimage to the summit of the mountain, on the last Sunday of the month, in honour of St Patrick. The great views impress even non-believers. July.

Puck Fair is set in Killorglin on the Ring of Kerry. This ancient festival is an excuse for drinking and carousing. August.

Galway Arts Festival is a mammoth celebration of theatre, film, art, literature and music overlapping with the races. Late July/August.

Rose of Tralee is a beauty pageant with a difference – internationally famous, it is accompanied by street parades and merrymaking. Tralee. August.

Fleadh Ceoil Na h'Éireann is held at various venues. Ireland's premier cultural festival; formal competition mixes with street entertainment and *craic*. August.

Kilkenny Arts Week is a wonderful festival of theatre and music, with events staged in pubs and a variety of small improvised venues all over town. August.

Match-Making Festival in Lisdoonvarna, Co Clare, is the place for bachelors and spinsters to seek out a spouse. Much more fun than computer dating. August.

September–October

Searching For That Elusive Irish Ancestor annual family history conference focusing on practical research in the main archives in Ireland. Includes lectures, tours and entertainment. Dublin and Belfast. September.

Oyster festivals are held in Galway and Clarinbridge.

Hurling and Gaelic football finals at Croke Park, Dublin.

Cork Film Festival is so popular that special ferries run between Britain and the Republic. September.

Waterford Festival of Light Opera is concerned with light opera and less prestigious than the Wexford opera festival, but all the more fun for it. October.

Ballinasloe October Fair, Co Galway is one of Ireland's oldest livestock markets, selling cattle and horses. October.

Dublin Theatre Festival. September/October.

Guinness Cork Jazz Festival hosts international stars performing all forms of jazz. September/October.

Kinsale Gourmet Festival is the country's best food festival. Kinsale restaurants offer a series of wonderful brunches and dinners in the heart of the old fishing village. October.

Wexford Festival Opera is Ireland's premier opera event. October.

The Dublin Marathon is usually staged in October. Anyone who thinks they are fit enough is welcome to join in.

November–December

Hunting, shooting and rugby seasons begin around this time.

Christmas is celebrated with gusto.

The Wren Boys, dressed as chimney sweeps with blacked faces, sing and perform in several Irish cities to raise money for charity each year on 26 December.

Left: comparing sounds, Ballina

Practical
Information

GETTING THERE

By Air

Dublin airport handles flights from Europe whilst most transatlantic flights arrive at Shannon airport. There are frequent flights to both airports and considerable competition between the airlines, including the Irish carriers Aer Lingus and Ryanair. It is well worth shopping around for low-cost fares and fly/drive packages.

Competitive prices are available on all UK–Ireland routes, and booking online is usually cheaper. BMI/British Midland (www.fly-bmi.com; tel: 0870-6070555) flies to Dublin from London Heathrow and East Midlands, and British Airways (tel: 0870 850 9850; www.britishairways.com) flies from London Gatwick. Ryanair (tel: 0871-2460000; www.ryanair.com) offers economy flights, from London's Stansted and Luton airports. Aer Lingus (tel: 0845-0844444; www.aerlingus.com) serves Dublin, Cork and Shannon. Aer Lingus' Irish flights connect with most major cities in the US and Europe.

From Dublin Airport, the Airlink bus connects with the city centre, bus and rail stations every 20 minutes. A taxi to the centre costs around €20–25.

By Sea

Irish Ferries operates from the UK port of Holyhead on the Isle of Anglesea to Dublin (tel: 08705-171717; www.irishferries.com). Swift operates four daily sailings between Dublin and Holyhead in 1 hour 49 minutes. Irish Ferries also links Pembroke and Rosslare, on the southeast coast. Stena Line (tel: 08705-707070; www.stenaline.ie) runs their Stena High-speed Service (99 minutes; takes vehicles) between Holyhead and Dun Laoghaire, south of Dublin.

North Merchant Ferries (UK tel: 0870-6004321; Ireland tel: 01-8192999) operates two 7½-hour overnight Liverpool–Dublin sailings a day.

Left: drive carefully
Right: life in the slow lane

Travelling to Ireland by ordinary (non-high-speed) ferry is slow (the crossing to Dublin takes a minimum of 3 hours). Again, it is worth shopping around and comparing the costs of a fly/drive package with those of ferry services.

TRAVEL ESSENTIALS

When to Visit

Some of the castles, gardens and museums of most interest are closed from the end of September until Easter, so it is best to visit in the main Easter to September season. Gardens and the flora of the Burren are at their best in June, while July and August are the busiest months, when hotels and restaurants are fullest. Oyster-lovers may prefer to visit in September when the new oyster season is celebrated in the Galway area.

Visas and Passports

Passports are required of everyone visiting the Republic except for UK citizens. Visas are not required by citizens of EU countries, Australia, New Zealand or the USA.

Vaccinations and Health

No vaccinations are required. EU citizens should obtain and file an E111 form to receive free medical care. Non-EU citizens are advised to take out health insurance.

Customs

Duty-free allowances (no longer available to travellers between EU countries) are 200 cigarettes, 1 litre of spirits, 2 litres of wine, 50 grams of perfume and ¼ litre of toilet water. With regard to **duty-paid** goods, EU members can take in up to 110 litres of beer, 90 litres of wine and 800 cigarettes. Special rules govern the import of most plant and food products.

Weather

Ireland receives a lot of rain because the prevailing southwesterly winds bring fronts in from the Atlantic. On the other hand the climate is mild, even in winter, because of the warming effects of the Gulf Stream.

Snow covers the higher mountains in winter, but prolonged frost is rare, so that many sub-tropical plants can flourish in Ireland.

Clothing

Dublin is both a casual and a formal city. women are extremely smart; men conflictingly underdressed. For the country, bring comfortable, preferably waterproof, footwear. Strong, water-resistant leather shoes/boots are best; Wellington boots are very useful.

Clothing should be windproof and waterproof to handle the inevitable showers and the quickly changing weather thrown in from the Atlantic. Sweaters and cardigans are a must. Dining at all levels is casual but smart; men are expected to wear a jacket and tie in top restaurants.

GETTING ACQUAINTED

Electricity

The standard electric current is 230 Volts, 50 cycles. Most hotels have 110-Volt shaver sockets. Wall sockets are three-pin flat or two-pin round.

Time Difference

Ireland observes Greenwich Mean Time in the winter; from the end of March to the end of September, clocks are 1 hour ahead of GMT.

Geography

Ireland is the most westerly nation in Europe and measures 275km (171 miles) at its greatest width and 468km (302 miles) from north to south. The saw-toothed coastline accounts for some 3,173km (1,970 miles) of beaches, inlets, cliffs and coves.

The island consists of an undulating central plain with varying soils, extensively covered with peat bog, a fifth of which is drained by the Shannon river basin. Surrounding the country completely is a broken chain of mountains. Waters from the Gulf Stream maintain a mild and equable climate, normally with a very heavy rainfall.

Government & Economy

The Republic of Ireland enjoys a parliamentary democracy within the EU. The Parliament *(Oireachtas)* consists of the President of the Nation *(Uachtarán nah hÉireann)* and two houses: an elected House of Representatives *(Dáil Éireann)* and a Senate *(Seanad Éireann)*. The president, currently Mary McAleese, is elected by a direct vote of the people for a seven-year term. General elections take place every five years. Elected members of *Dáil Éireann* use the initials TD after their names.

The Irish economy relies heavily on trade with other members of the European Union, especially the UK. Agriculture is no longer the most important sector of the economy, although it still accounts for 10 percent of the country's GDP.

Ireland, with its educated workforce, was extremely successful in the 1990s in attracting foreign investment in manufacturing electronics, computers, pharmaceuticals, machinery and transport equipment. The

Above: flying the flag

economic miracle performed by the 'Celtic tiger' couldn't last for ever, of course, and recent global downturns in trade have restored a sense of reality.

MONEY MATTERS

From 1 January 2002, the Republic of Ireland adopted the euro (€) as its currency and the old Irish pound (or punt) ceased to be legal tender the following month.

Banknotes come in denominations of €5, €10, €20, €50, €100, €200 and €500. Coins come in denominations of 1 cent, 2¢, 5¢, 10¢, 20¢, 50¢, €1 and €2.

Bank hours are Monday to Friday 10am–4pm, with one day late opening until 5pm (Thur in Dublin). Smaller town banks may close for lunch from 12.30–1.30pm.

Traveller's cheques are one of the safest ways of carrying money. If lost or stolen, cheques can be replaced, usually within 24 hours in the case of American Express.

Across the border in Northern Ireland, the British pound (£) is the standard currency, though most traders in border areas are prepared to accept euros.

Tipping

Tipping is not expected in bars. However, it is usual to give a 10 percent tip in taxis and restaurants. Be aware that some hotels and restaurants automatically add a fixed service charge to your bill.

GETTING AROUND

Driving

A car is essential in order to follow the itineraries in this book. If you are not bringing your own car over by ferry, you should investigate fly/drive packages offered by the major airlines, or you can rent a car on arrival at Shannon or Dublin airport. Car hire is more expensive than in the UK or Continental Europe – but prices vary greatly according to season.

Documents

To drive your own car in Ireland, you need comprehensive insurance valid for Ireland and a driving licence. To rent a car, you need a full valid licence of your own country

Right: 'May the road rise to meet you'

(which you must have held for at least two years) or an international licence. The minimum hiring age differs according to the hire company.

Rules

Traffic drives on the left. Seat belts must be worn by the driver and front-seat passenger. Children must travel in the rear. Drink driving laws are very strict – it is best not to drink if you intend to drive. The speed limit on open roads is 97kmh (60mph); in built-up areas it is 65kmh (40mph), in towns and villages 50kmh (30mph). The motorway limit is 113 kmh (70mph).

General

The Republic of Ireland consists of 26 counties and Northern Ireland (part of the United Kingdom) of six. Most of the higher ground lies close to the coast, while the Midlands tend to be flat, and are often covered by bog. In the thinly populated west of Ireland, roads tend to be of poorer quality. Travelling Ireland's highways and byways can sometimes be a hair-raising experience. Some Irish people drive with a devil-may-care attitude and appear not to recognise anything so mundane as a speed limit. Drive with caution.

On country roads, beware of cattle, sheep, dogs, tractors and pedestrians.

In the *Gaeltacht* (Irish Gaelic-speaking areas) many signs will be in Irish only, as

is the case on the Dingle Peninsula and in parts of Galway.

Maps

A good set of maps (such as the Irish Ordnance Survey's 1:250,000 *Holiday Map* series) is essential, since it is a national pastime to remove or redirect road signs.

HOLIDAYS AND HOURS

Shops generally open 9am–5.30pm Monday to Saturday. Most rural towns have half-day closing, when shops are shut for one afternoon a week; the day varies from place to place. In cities and larger towns shops stay open until 9pm one day a week – usually on Friday. In Killarney, the tourist capital of Ireland, shops stay open until 10pm in the summer and in the cities there are 24-hour shops. *(For bank hours see Money Matters, page 85).*

Bars, pubs and taverns open Monday to Wednesday 10.30am–11.30am; Thursday to Saturday 10.30am–12.30am; Sun 12.30–11pm (with 30 minutes' drinking-up time).

Public holidays are:
1 January
17 March (St Patrick's Day)
Good Friday
Easter Monday
1st Monday in May
1st Monday in June
1st Monday in August

Last Monday in October
25–26 December

ACCOMMODATION

The ratings used in the guide refer to the cost of a double room (with Irish breakfast):

€€€€ = Very Expensive (over €250)
€€€ = Expensive (over €150)
€€ = Moderate (over €100)
€ = Inexpensive (under €100).

It is advisable to book your accommodation in advance for Dublin, and for all locations between June and the end of September. Reservations can be made through any Irish Tourist Board *(Bord Fáilte)* office for a small fee to cover telephone costs and a 10 percent deposit.

Visitors will be inundated with different accommodation guides, all sold at tourist offices and bookshops. The most comprehensive is *Be Our Guest* by the Irish Hotels Federation. There are also specific booklets: *Ireland's Blue Book* (exclusive country house hotels and restaurants); *Farmhouse Accommodation*; *Friendly Homes of Ireland* (family guest houses); and *The Hidden Ireland* (family-run manors or country houses where you may be paying as much for ambience as accommodation). In many cases dinner is also offered (prior notice required). *Bord Fáilte* has various information booklets on self-catering, camping and hostels.

Dublin

The art of innkeeping seems to come naturally to Dubliners. This city, one of the smallest European capitals, has a surprising number of luxury hotels, and the tourist boom of the late 1990s resulted in a good many new hotels being built.

The Clarence
6–8 Wellington Quay, Dublin 2
Tel: 01-407 0800. €€€€
www.theclarence.ie
Located within walking distance of the centre of town, this stylish hotel, owned by members of the rock group U2, has Art Deco rooms and a lovely restaurant.

Left: Longfield's Hotel, Dublin

Grand Canal Hotel
Grand Canal Street, Ballsbridge, Dublin 4
Tel: 01-646 1000. €€
New hotel in the heart of Dublin's up and coming quayside district. Near the DART station.

King Sitric
East Pier, Howth, Co Dublin
Tel: 01-832 5235 €
This renowned fish restaurant has eight cosy rooms, many with excellent sea views.

Longfield's Hotel
9–10 Lower Fitzwilliam Street, Dublin 2
Tel: 01-676 1367. €€€
www.longfields.ie
Small cosy hotel in southside Georgian area. Good food in basement restaurant.

The Oliver St John Gogarty
Anglesea Street, Temple Bar, Dublin 2
Tel: 01-671 1822. €
www.gogartys.ie
A recent addition to the budget accommodation market, offering bright, airy rooms in the heart of trendy Temple Bar.

The Shelbourne
27 St Stephen's Green, Dublin 2
Tel: 01-663 4500. €€€€
A grand hotel where the Constitution was drafted. The rooms may be cramped but the surroundings are elegant. Delightful, formal bars – great for afternoon tea or drinks.

Temple Bar Hotel
Fleet Street, Temple Bar, Dublin 2
Tel: 01-677 3333. €€
www.templebarhotel.com
Cheerful hotel with restaurants. Convenient for both Temple Bar and business quarter.

The Westbury
Grafton Street, Dublin 2
Tel: 01-679 1122. €€€€
Modern international hotel well located in the heart of the shopping district – very convenient for Trinity College.

Donegal to Sligo

Central Hotel
The Diamond, Donegal, Co Donegal
Tel: 074-972 1027. €€
In the very centre of town. A good place to participate in the local social life. Rooms overlooking the bay.

Clarence Hotel
Wine Street, Sligo, Co Sligo
Tel: 071-9142211. €€
Centrally located and family-run.

Green Gate
Adara, Co Donegal
Tel: 074 9541546. €
This set of hill-top farm cottages now comprises one of Ireland's best B&Bs and a modern entry to a tradition of monastic retreats.

St Ernan's House
Donegal, Co Donegal
Tel: 074-9721065. €€€€
Deluxe hotel on an island, connected by a causeway, with lovely views of the bay, and a superb menu. Easter–Oct.

Markree Castle
Collooney, Co Sligo.
Tel: 071 9167800. €€€
www.markreecastle.ie
Imposing pre-Cromwellian castle turned into a hotel. Salmon fishing is available on the river in the estate. Also has a very good restaurant.

The Far West

Delphi Lodge
Leenane, Co Galway
Tel: 095 42222. €€€
www.delphilodge.ie
This grand historic home modestly calls itself a fishing lodge. Indeed the nearby mountain lakes and streams are an angler's dream, but one could be forgiven for coming just for the fantastic evening meals served around the large dining room table. Call for directions.

Hotel Clew Bay
James Street, Westport, Co Mayo
Tel: 098-28088. €€
www.clewbayhotel.com
Small family-run hotel with an excellent restaurant overlooking the Carrowbeg River.

Dromoland Castle
Newmarket-on-Fergus, Co Clare
Tel: 061-368144. €€€€
www.dromoland.ie

Set in the ancestral home of Conor O'Brien, descendant of Brian Ború who defeated the Vikings in 1014. The hotel has enormous antique-filled rooms, splendid views over the estate, golf course and majestic dining room.

County Galway
Galway City
Galway Great Southern
Eyre Square, Galway, Co Galway
Tel: 091-564041. €€€€
www.gshotels.com
Nineteenth-century railway hotel with Victorian ambience, but provides mod cons, such as the heated rooftop pool. The Oyster Room restaurant is Galway's most elegant dining room.

Skeffington Arms
28 Eyre Square, Galway, Co Galway
Tel: 091-563173. €€
www.skeffington.ie
Historic hotel in the heart of the city.

Star of the Sea
125 Upper Salthill, Galway
Tel: 091 525900. €
www.astarofthesea.com
This is one of the better options in Salthill's burgeoning B&B market. Good view of the bay and near the high street's facilities.

Clifden
Abbeyglen Castle Hotel
Sky Road, Clifden, Co Galway

Tel: 095-22832. €€€
www.abbeyglen.ie
Gourmet cuisine; specialities usually include oysters and lobster; piano music; panoramic views of Clifden and the sea.

The Quay House
Beach Road, Clifden, Co Galway
Tel: 095-21369. €€
Small friendly hotel 10 minutes from the centre of Clifden, overlooking the harbour.

Rock Glen Country House Hotel
Clifden, Co Galway
Tel: 095-21035. €€
Country-life atmosphere in a converted hunting lodge. The hotel also has a good restaurant serving fresh local produce.

County Limerick
Limerick City
Clarion Hotel Limerick
Steamboat Quay, Limerick
Tel: 021-4908298. €€
www.clarionhotellimerick.com
Ireland's tallest hotel and one that combines luxury with affordabilty and a relaxed staff.

Adare
Adare Manor
Adare, Co Limerick
Tel: 061-396566. €€€–€€€€
www.adaremanor.com
Luxurious country house hotel set in a vast Victorian Gothic pile. Huge, antique-furnished rooms, swimming pool, spa, riding, fishing, golf (on the Manor's fine Robert Trent Jones course), and live musical entertainment nightly in summer.

County Kerry
Killarney
19th Green
Lackabane, Fossa, Killarney, Co Kerry
Tel: 064-32868. €
www.19thgreen-bb.com
Family run guesthouse just outside of Killarney. Ideal location for golfers – there are six nearby courses to choose from.

Tralee
Ballygarry House
Killarney Road, Tralee, Co Kerry
Tel: 066-7123322. €€

Above: an Irish welcome

www.ballygarryhouse.com
Comfortable hotel with a restaurant serving fresh local food.

Brandon Inn
James Street, Tralee, Co Kerry
Tel: 066-7129666. €€
www.brandonhotel.ie
Modern central hotel, with swimming pool and restaurant.

Ballyseede Castle
Ballyseede, Tralee, Co Kerry
Tel: 066-7125799. €€€
www.ballyseedecastle.com
Small hotel (13 rooms) of great character.

County Cork
Cork City
Arbutus Lodge Hotel
Saint Luke's, Cork, Co Cork
Tel: 021-4501237. €€
Atmospheric late 18th-century hotel with a Michelin-starred restaurant; superb, inventive seafood dishes are the speciality of the house, but you can also enjoy an inexpensive lunch in the Gallery Bistro.

Bantry
Eccles Hotel
Glengarriff Harbour, Bantry, Co Cork
Tel: 027-63003. €€
www.eccleshotel.com
A grand, if slightly shabby, seafront hotel that once welcomed Queen Victoria as a guest. It has a reasonably good seafood restaurant and an old-fashioned bar warmed by a cosy log fire.

Kinsale
Cottage Loft
6 Main Street, Kinsale, Co Cork
Tel: 021-4772803. €
Guesthouse accommodation, with restaurant offering gourmet cuisine by gifted local owner/chef; low-key but charming setting; specialities include seafood.

Kieran's Folkhouse Inn
Guardwell, Kinsale, Co Cork
Tel: 021-4772382. €
Snug seafaring inn, with cosy bars and a restaurant offering lively, inventive dishes.

Skibbereen
West Cork Hotel
Ilen Street, Skibbereen, Co Cork
Tel: 028-21277 €€€
www.westcorkhotel.com
Atmospheric old railway hotel which offers excellent food. Guests are guaranteed a warm Irish welcome.

County Waterford
Waterford
Athenaeum House Hotel
Christendom, Ferrybank, Waterford
Tel: 051-833999. €€
This estate home is only minutes' drive from Waterford city centre, but seems like it's in the middle of the countryside.

The Granville
Meagher Quay, Waterford, Co Waterford
Tel: 051-305555. €€€
www.granvillehotel.ie
Traditional but sombre hotel with good restaurant and central location.

Waterford Castle
The Island, Ballinakill, Co Waterford
Tel: 051-878203. €€€€
www.waterfordcastle.com
This Fitzgerald family castle, built in the 17th century, stands on an island reached by ferry just outside Waterford. Four-poster beds and a strong sense of history are complemented by a good restaurant serving traditional Irish food. There is an 18-hole golf course and driving range, and tennis court.

County Kilkenny
Maddoxtown
Blanchville House
Dunbell, Maddoxtown, Co Kilkenny
Tel: 056-7727197. €–€€
www.blanchville.ie
Warm hospitality in a period country house 8km (5 miles) from Kilkenny.

County Wexford
Wexford
The Talbot Hotel
Trinity Street, Wexford, Co Wexford
Tel: 053-23377. €€€
www.talbothotel.ie
Lively, comfortable hotel. Restaurant and bar food, indoor pool and leisure centre.

Newbay Country House
Co Wexford
Tel: 053-42779. €
www.newbayhouse.com
Elegant family-run Georgian mansion set
in parkland 3km (2 miles) from Wexford town.

County Wicklow

Brook Lodge
Macreddin Village, near Aughrim
Tel: 0402 364444. €€€
A unique experience in Irish accommoda-
tion. Macreddin Village is a creation for Brook
Lodge and includes a pub and two restau-
rants. The lodge is luxury accommodation
with an in-house spa to help guests relax.

EMERGENCIES

For any of the emergency services (police,
fire or ambulance) dial 999 or 112.

Ireland has little serious crime, but there
is the usual petty theft and you should lock
away or conceal valuables. In Dublin, especially, use official car parks.

For medical or dental services, consult
your hotel in the first instance; they will be
able to recommend or call out a local doctor/
dentist. Medical and dental services are of
a high standard. European Union visitors
receive free medical services provided they
have completed a form E111.

COMMUNICATIONS & NEWS

Post
Postage stamps are sold by all
post offices, plus some souvenir
shops and general stores. Post office hours are Mon–Fri 9am–
5.30pm, Sat 9am–1pm.

Telephones
Public telephones are mostly card
phones (cards cost €4, €7 or €15).
Coin-operated phones accept 10¢,
20¢, 50¢, €1 and €2 coins. The
minimum charge for a call is 40¢.
Card phones are cheaper than pay
phones. Visa cards can be used in
most public phones but cost 60¢
extra per call.

For directory enquiries dial 190; for international assistance dial 114. To dial other
countries, dial the international access code
00, then the country code: e.g. UK (44); US
and Canada (1). Ireland's access code from
overseas is 353. If using a US phone credit
card, dial the company's access number below – Sprint, tel: 1-800-552-001; AT&T, tel:
1-800-550- 000; MCI, tel: 1-800-551-001.

Media
The national broadcasting service, Radio
Telefís Éireann, has three TV channels (one,
TG4, broadcasting exclusively in Irish
Gaelic) and three radio stations. TV3, Ire-
land's first independent television network,
was launched in 1998. Britain's BBC1,
BBC2, ITV1 and Channel 4 are also avail-
able, as are satellite and cable. RTE Radio
1 is the main news and current affairs station,
while RTE 2 broadcasts mostly pop music.
There are also many independent stations.

Dublin's main newspapers are the *Irish
Times* and the *Irish Independent*. There are
also regional papers, Sunday papers and all
the British papers. *In Dublin*, a bi-monthly
listings magazine, is worth buying.

LANGUAGE

The language of everyday use is English,
even though Irish Gaelic is the official language. English is relatively new here, having been forcibly introduced in 1831 to
wither Irish national identity.

Irish Gaelic is a Celtic language related to
Breton, Cornish and Welsh, and much more
closely related to Scots Gaelic and Manx,
with a special alphabet that has distinct and
beautiful characters. Today it is encouraged
and taught in schools. Many people in the
western areas known as the *Gaeltacht* speak
Irish Gaelic as their first tongue.

SPORT

Hurling, an ancient game considered the
fastest field sport in the world, and Gaelic football are played across Ireland at weekends.

Hurling, reputed to be the sport of Irish
heroes many centuries ago, is played by men
(the related game of Camogie is played by
women) and is a 15-a-side team game. Play-

Left: one of Ireland's 40 shades of green

ers hit a small leather-covered ball with a 'hurley stick' made of ash, which has a curved blade at its end. Like soccer, the object is to score goals. Gaelic football is also a 15-a-side game best described as a blending of rugby and soccer.

The 'sport of kings', horse racing, is synonymous with Ireland, which is also renowned for breeding winners. Wherever you are in the country, you are never far away from a county racecourse where you can join in the excitement on a Sunday afternoon.

TOURS

With careful planning, some of the itineraries in this guide can be covered on public transport. As a break from driving, you might consider taking a bus tour. Such organised tours are available from Cork, Galway, Killarney and Tralee tourist offices. Also call Bus Éireann (tel: 01-8366111). Most tours operate only in summer, but in Killarney, Dero's also runs tours out-of-season (tel: 064-31251).

USEFUL ADDRESSES

Tourist offices

The Irish Tourist Board (*Bord Fáilte*), has offices in most towns. They not only supply information but also act as travel agents: you can use them to book accommodation, tours, car rental, tickets and so on.

They will also supply information on sport, diving, golf, cycling, fishing and any other type of special-interest activity. Finally, all have a *Bureau de Change* and a shop selling maps, books and quality handicrafts.

A complete list of all offices is available from any *Bord Fáilte* office in Ireland or worldwide. The following regional offices are open year-round:

Cork	021-4255100
Dingle	066-9151188
Dublin City	01-6057700
Ennis	065-6828366
Galway	091-537700
Kilkenny	056-7751500
Killarney	064-31633
Kinsale	021-4772234
Limerick	061-317522

Sligo	071-9161201
Tralee	066-7121288
Waterford	051-875823
Westport	098-25711
Wexford	053-23111
Wicklow	0404-69117

Dúchas, the heritage service, offers a yearly pass, which is good value if you plan to visit a lot of sites: for €20 (adult) €7.50 (child), or €50 (family), you can have unlimited access to all 100-plus sites managed by Dúchas. You can buy the card at the first site you visit, or contact them for details:

Heritage Card Officer
6 Upper Ely Place
FREEPOST
Dublin 2
Tel: 01 647 2461
www.heritageireland.ie
heritagecard@duchas.ie

FURTHER READING

Ardagh, John. *Ireland and the Irish: Portrait of a Changing Society*. Penguin.

Beckett, J.C. *The Making of Modern Ireland*. Faber.

Bell, Brian (ed). *Insight Guide: Ireland*, and *Insight Guide Dublin*. Apa Publications.

Doyle, Roddy. *Dublin Trilogy*.

Delany, Frank. *James Joyce's Odyssey – A Guide to the Dublin of Ulysses*. Hodder & Stoughton.

Gogarty, Oliver St John. *As I Was Going Down Sackville Street*. Sphere.

Harbison, Peter. *Guide to National and Historic Monuments in Ireland*. Gill and Macmillan.

Joyce, James. *Ulysses* and *Dubliners*.

Jeffares and Kamm (eds). *Irish Childhoods* (*an anthology*). Gill and Macmillan.

Kee, Robert. *Ireland – A History*. Weidenfeld.

Keneally, Thomas. *Now and In the Time to Be*. Flamingo.

Murphy, Dervla. *Ireland*. Salem House.

O'Faolain Sean. *The Irish: A Character Study*. Penguin Books.

Somerville-Large, Peter. *Dublin*. Hamish Hamilton and *The Coast of West Cork*. Appletree. Hamilton.

ACKNOWLEDGEMENTS

Photography	
5, 7 (top), 11, 12, 31, 33, 37, 49, 50,	**Marcus Wilson Smith**
57 (bottom) 59, 61, 63, 67 (top),	
72, 82, 84	
6, 21, 25, 27, 28, 30, 34, 36, 39, 40, 41	**Guy Mansell**
52 (top), 54 (top), 60 (top), 66	
67 (bottom), 79, 85, 88, 90	
1, 7 (bottom), 8/9, 14, 20, 23, 24, 26, 43	**Geray Sweeney**
45, 47, 53, 54 (bottom), 55, 56	
57 (bottom), 58, 69, 70, 75, 76, 77, 86	
60 (bottom)	**Bord Fáilte**
Back Cover	**Brian Harris**
16	**Brian Harris/Alamy**
46, 71	**Brian Lynch**
78	**Toby Melville/Reuters/Corbis**
15	**Richard Nowitz**
52 (bottom)	**Office of Public Works**
2/3	**Tony Stone Images**
Cover	**Stone/Joe Cornish**
10	**Trinity College Dublin**
Cartography	**Berndtson & Berndtson**
	Mike Larby

© APA Publications GmbH & Co. Verlag KG Singapore Branch, Singapore

INDEX